I Wish Someone Had Told Me

I Wish Someone Had Told Me

Exploring Essential Elements of the Christian Faith

An In-Depth 10-Week Bible Study Guide

by

Barbie Loflin

WordCrafts

I Wish Someone Had Told Me
Copyright © 2016
Barbie Loflin

Unless otherwise noted all Scripture quotations are taken from THE HOLY BIBLE, NEW INTERNATIONAL VERSION®, NIV® Copyright © 1973, 1978, 1984, 2011 by Biblica, Inc.™ Used by permission. All rights reserved worldwide.

Scripture quotations marked "Message" are from THE MESSAGE. Copyright © by Eugene H. Peterson 1993, 1994, 1995, 1996, 2000, 2001, 2002. Used by permission of Tyndale House Publishers, Inc.

Scripture quotations marked "AB" taken from the Amplified®Bible, Copyright © 1954, 1958, 1962, 1964, 1965, 1987 by The Lockman Foundation. Used by permission." (www.Lockman.org)

Scripture quotations marked "TLB" are taken from The Living Bible copyright © 1971. Used by permission of Tyndale House Publishers, Inc., Carol Stream, Illinois 60188. All rights reserved.

Scripture quotations marked "KJV" are from the King James Version of The Holy Bible, public domain.

Cover design by David Warren

All rights reserved. No part of this book may be reproduced, stored in a retrieval system, or transmitted in any form or by any means – electronic, mechanical, photocopy, recording, or otherwise – without the prior written permission of the publisher. The only exception is brief quotations for review purposes

Published by WordCrafts Press
Buffalo, Wyoming 82834
www.wordcrafts.net

Dedication

To Aaron, my brave and laughing Levite,
Matthew, my quick-witted genius,
and Kayti, my beautiful dancing drama queen.
My babies. My teachers.
You have changed everything I ever believed about love.
How blessed I am to have been given
the privilege of sharing your lives.
My prayer is that each of you will live lives
extravagantly wrapped in Jesus.

You take my breath away.

My Heart

I am a firm believer in deep and passionate pursuit.

I never want to live my life without it. I am absolutely convinced that we, God's Daughters, were never intended to live a dry passionless existence, but were created with a fiery love burning inside of us for the One Who breathed life into us.

Whether washing His feet with our tears, or running to tell everyone we have seen Him, our history in the earth has been one of great passion. We are marked by and come alive in those moments when everything inside of us awakens and moves, our spirits being deeply stirred by the very heartbeat of God.

We, the daughters, are of the ones who stayed at the cross, and the ones who first shared the news of His resurrection. Why do you think we were afforded such a privilege? Perhaps it was because He knew we could not stay away from Him long enough for someone else to find out first. We were just that in love with Him.

We are the hungry, the pursuing, the passionate Bride of Christ, and we should live as nothing less.

I want more than anything else to let women everywhere know how extravagantly they are loved, and how lavishly they can love in return. My heart's desire is to live my life faithfully, compelling others to live in fullest service to, and with greatest passion for, Their Beloved.

For truly, His is an all-consuming love.

Forward

The house is finally quiet. The children have fallen asleep after a full day of swimming, climbing, sandboxes, tire swings and general mayhem. I think they all passed the tired point about two hours ago, but waited for exhaustion to carry them into the oblivion of sleep. I love this time of night. It is my time to reflect. My time to look back on the day and all that I have learned; to count my blessings, so to speak.

I pick up a Barbie doll from the living room floor, convinced that I will find her clothes just around the corner. A soccer ball staggers across the floor as my fuzzy slipper accidentally nudges it from its resting place, the center of the living room floor. I turn to pick the ball up and trip over my son's little sneakers – size 13s that look more like speed bumps than shoes. Still calm. Still reflecting on the day.

My findings deposited safely in the appropriate rooms, I venture into the kitchen, the hub of the Loflin household. This is where we congregate, share meals, talk about school and work. I run my hand across the counter, chasing a family of dust bunnies that moved in and seem determined to stay. The family cat, Molly, circles my feet, mewing as she begs for the food that will sustain her – giving her yet another opportunity to cough up fur balls during my dinner parties. I stack a few dishes in the dishwasher as I try to remember what it was I had forgotten to do this evening. My husband calls from the other room. I remember what it was I had forgotten.

The house is finally quiet. I sit down in front of my computer; all of the thoughts I had saved just for this moment begin to saunter through my mind. My fingers finally touch the keyboard…

I awaken with the imprint of a semi-colon on my forehead.

I offer this time and this study to you, my precious Lord and Savior, Jesus Christ. It is because of You that I am compelled to share this ministry through written word. You so fill my heart that I can scarce contain all You have given me. I pray that You touch everyone who walks this path with me. May they be enlightened by Your Word, wooed by Your Holy Spirit, and set free by the Truth of Who You are.

Table of Contents

I Wish Someone Had Told Me Perfection is a Process 1
- Perfect Grace 3
- Perfect Growth 8
- Perfect Wisdom 12
- Perfect Mercy 17
- Perfect Love 21

I Wish Someone Had Told Me What it Means to be Faithful 27
- Faithfulness of God 29
- Faithfulness of God 34
- God's Faithfulness, Continued 38
- Faithfulness to Commitments 43
- Faithfulness in Marriage 48

I Wish Someone Had Told Me I Am Fearfully and Wonderfully Made 55
- In the Beginning 57
- The Weight of the World 62
- Losing Yourself 67
- What About Me? 72
- Better Things 76

I Wish Someone Had Told Me About Worship 80
- The Exchange 82
- It is Just Your Life 87
- To Praise Him 91
- In the Assembly 96
- Just Between You and Me 101

I Wish Someone Had Told Me Marriage Is Hard Work 106
- Knight in Shining Armor 108
- What Do You Think? 114
- Reality and Fantasy 119
- The Word on Marriage 123
- Putting It All Together 126

I Wish Someone Had Told Me About Satan's Mind Games 133
- Footholds 135
- Strongholds 139
- Confusion and a Double Mind 146
- Dread, Worry and Torment 151
- A Sound Mind 155

I Wish Someone Had Told Me Falling Only Counts When You Do Not Get Up 160
- The Biggest Failures 162
- The Biggest Failures…cont. 166
- Beams and Splinters 172
- Letting Go 176
- Restoration 180

I Wish Someone Had Told Me It is Possible to Continually Know the Peace of God 185
- When You Seek Me 187
- Peace Like a River 191
- Entering His Rest 196
- The Whirlwind 200
- In That Day 205

I Wish Someone Had Told Me God is my Only Constant 211
- Changing Times 213
- Changing Seasons 217
- Changing Plans 222
- Changing Relationships 226
- Changing Hearts 233

I Wish Someone Had Told Me All Things are Possible with God 240
- Childish Dreams 242
- New Hopes 246
- Setting Goals 251
- Mountain Moving 255
- Dare To Dream 260

Week One

I Wish Someone Had Told Me Perfection is a Process

"Be perfect, therefore, as your Heavenly Father is perfect."

Matthew 5:48

Day 1
Perfect Grace

Day 2
Perfect Growth

Day 3
Perfect Wisdom

Day 4
Perfect Mercy

Day 5
Perfect Love

This week's lesson will deal with the pursuit of perfection. I can hear the groans as I type the words! Some are thinking, 'This week is definitely not for me, I gave up a long time ago!' Still, others are thinking, 'If I could only fix this specific part of my life everything really would be perfect.' Whatever your gut response may be, let's take some time this week to find out what the Word of God says about our relentless pursuits. What does He think about our goals and our plans? Is He our driving force, or are we simply driving ourselves? Are we seeking a perfect heart or a perfect life? God has planned our perfection from the beginning. He is the only One capable of bringing it to pass. Be released into the Master Potter's hand this week and allow Him to do what He does best - perfect that which concerns you.

> *The Lord will accomplish that which concerns me; Your [unwavering] lovingkindness, O Lord, endures forever. Do not abandon the works of Your own hands.*
>
> Psalm 138:8 (AB)

Day 1

Perfect Grace

"I always thank my God for you because of his grace given you in Christ Jesus. For in him you have been enriched in every way – with all kinds of speech and with all knowledge –"

1 Corinthians 1:4, 5

I am a preacher's kid.

Perfect. Preacher's kid. Perfect. They both start with a 'P' but that is about the only similarity you will find. Someone should have mentioned this to me years ago. It might have saved me endless hours of frustration as well as feelings of failure and inadequacy. The Apostle Paul describes my walk with Christ in all of its blazing glory in the 7th chapter of Romans. Read the following verses and see if they do not accurately portray at least a portion (probably a great portion, if you are like me) of your life.

Read Romans 7:18-25

From this passage of scripture, write the verse that most accurately describes the struggles you have experienced in your Christian walk.

_____
_____
_____
_____

Keep in mind that there is no wrong answer, but I have a sneaking suspicion that 98 percent of you have written verse 19. Why? Because we are walking around in flesh and blood bodies and these bodies really like to have their own way. The battle between our flesh and our spirit is constant. Look again at verses 22 and 23. Sounds like a battle going on to me. If Paul struggled against his flesh, obviously losing that battle at times, why do we assume that if we just prayed a little harder, read the Word a little more, spent more time performing charitable acts, or teaching more Bible studies, we would be able to totally master this body? It is this assumption that causes many of us to live defeated Christian lives. We become so focused on our failures that we cannot see the progress we are making. Am I saying that sin is okay? Absolutely not! Paul addresses this very issue in Romans 6.

Let's look at the following scriptures.

Read Romans 6 (yes, the entire chapter)

What did Paul say about continuing to sin? (v. 1, 2)

_____
_____
_____
_____

What do you think Paul meant when he said we *died to sin*?

_____
_____
_____
_____

What instruction does he give us in verses 12 and 13?

_____
_____
_____
_____

How would you answer the question posed in verse 21?

_____
_____
_____
_____

Why all of the talk of sin and grace? The road to 'perfection' is paved with both. The only One who walked in perfection upon this earth was Jesus Christ. He arrived in perfection and maintained that state until the moment He ascended into the clouds to rejoin His Father. He remains beyond perfection throughout eternity. As for the rest of us, perfection is a process steeped in the grace of the Almighty. I guess now might be the appropriate time to let you off the hook just a bit. *Perfect*, in the Greek, is best defined as *mature*, and *mature* is defined as *fully developed* or *grown, completed*. We do not arrive at maturity overnight, just as we could never hope to attain perfection in this earthly body. We complete His call to perfection (maturity) on a daily basis. With this definition in mind, let's take a look at Matthew 5:48.

Do you think Jesus would ever tell us to do something that was impossible to do?

_____
_____
_____
_____

What do you think He is saying in this particular verse?

_____
_____
_____
_____

When we look at this verse in the context of the original text, we begin to see this command as an attainable promise instead of a condemning command. Jesus' words, when looked at closely, can bring comfort and hope. If He is telling me to grow in maturity, then I must be able to do just that!

Growth takes time, so God must be giving me time to grow.

How many of us (when our children began to walk) would chastise them when they stumbled? Silly isn't it? Of course, no loving parent would do that to a baby. We encourage and instruct, then encourage and instruct some more. Mixed in with all of this is a truckload of praise, and 'oohs' and 'aahs.' We stay in the process with that child until the lesson is completed. After the child learns to walk, we expect him to continue in that knowledge. We do not wake up in the morning wondering if that child will remember how to walk or if that child will choose to walk that day. We know that the child has learned well and expect him to use that lesson.

In the same manner, God takes a scriptural truth and places it before us. He instructs us and encourages us in that truth, then He instructs and encourages us some more. He stays with us, constantly speaking this truth to our hearts until we know it. We toddle around on legs that do not want to carry us where the scripture leads, and we cry and wail every time we stumble; still He encourages and instructs. Then one day He says, "Now, child, walk."

We have a choice to make in that moment. Will we walk in what we know to be truth, or will we sit down and refuse His instruction? Often times the destination set before us will determine whether or not we walk. How sad that is, for our heart's desire should not be the destination, but obedience to the One who holds destiny in His mighty hands.

Too many days are spent in pursuit of the destination. But then there are *Those Days* - days when all we want to do is walk where He has shown us to walk; days when our stubborn will bows to His loving instruction; days when being in His presence is our ultimate destination; days that take our breath away as we get tiny glimpses of the Awesome One who is teaching us to walk. These are the days when our spirits expand in the knowledge of Him and we find ourselves walking the well-lined, mature road of grace perfected.

In concluding today's lesson, I would like to leave you with a couple of questions.

How do you feel when you fail to be perfect?

_____
_____
_____
_____

Who or what gave you the idea that anything less than perfection would not be good enough for God?
_____
_____
_____
_____

How do you think God feels when you are not perfect?
_____
_____
_____
_____

Why do you think He feels that way? What scriptural proof can you give to back up your belief?
_____
_____
_____
_____

Questions or comments concerning today's lesson:

Day 2

Perfect Growth

"They will be called oaks of righteousness, a planting of the Lord for the display of his splendor."
Isaiah 61:3b

Have you ever really thought about being the *display of His splendor*? We take great care in dressing, choosing the appropriate attire for each occasion. We carefully apply makeup and accessories that will set off the clothing we have chosen. We wash our hair, using the best products, dry and style it, and check the mirror just one more time before we head out the door. And we do all of this for what? The display of our splendor. Yes, I believe God wants us to take care of our bodies and our appearance. I believe, though I struggle in this area, that God intends for us to be faithful stewards over the body He gave us; exercising it, feeding it properly and subduing it to the authority of Christ. This, however, was never intended to be our focus. We are to display *His* splendor.

A perfect example of incorrect focus would be the contrast between the time spent dressing for church on Sunday morning, as compared to the amount of prayer given concerning the actual service. While standing in front of the mirror one Sunday morning, yelling for the kids to hurry as I applied that all-important second coat of mascara (heavy sarcasm), I sensed the Holy Spirit trying to get my attention. You know how all of a sudden you begin to feel like something just is not quite right?

Are you ready? I thought to myself.

I perused my reflection. Yes; everything was painted, ironed and smelled good!

Are you ready? The thought ran through my mind again.

I stared into the mirror hoping to miss the flaws I knew I would find if I looked too intently. *Well, it is not going to get any better than this*, I thought.

Are you ready?

Yes! I am ready, already! I fussed to myself!

What about your heart?

What? I whispered.

Is your heart ready for service?

I thought for a moment about what I had done since awakening that morning. I had made breakfast, made beds, ironed a little pink dress, sipped my coffee, talked to my husband, I had even planned lunch. Now, here I was ready to walk out the door, and not once had I given thought to my Lord. Not once had I thanked Him for the privilege of being able to go to His house. Not once had I asked Him to be a part of my day, to forgive my sins and help me walk in the new mercies He gives every morning. I had not prepared my heart to enter into His house. I had merely been preparing to display myself, not Christ in me.

I would love to tell you that I stopped what I was doing, dropped to my knees and wept, but I did not. Instead, I began to think about the state of my heart and my priorities. I began to think about how I did things and why I did them the way that I did. I began to search my heart. Today's lesson encompasses some of the scriptures that came to light during this search.

My first question to the Lord was, *what am I supposed to be doing to display your splendor*? Which led me to wonder what His splendor is exactly, and what it means to display it?

Splendor is defined as "magnificence, grandeur or glory."

Display is defined as "a show or exhibition of something, done to impress the people."

I am called to make an exhibition of His glory that will impress the people. Coming from my background as a preacher's kid, I had a little bit of a problem with the thought of being "showy." I had been taught that we are to be humble, never to show-off. I am not saying that I have always lived by that creed, but I had been taught. As I pondered this displaying of glory in my heart, the Holy Spirit began to expand my thought process.

Read Colossians 2:9, then write it in the space provided.

_____
_____
_____
_____

Keep in mind the phrase "fullness of the Godhead, bodily."

Jesus was the fullest representation of God. He was God in bodily form. The glory of God was displayed in and through Christ Jesus. Therefore, it makes sense that if we are to display His glory, we must display Jesus. What was Jesus' ultimate goal? If I knew His purpose, then I would know my own. If I knew what His motivation was, then I would have my own. All I had to do was find out the first priority of Christ.

Read John 14:31. What did Jesus say He did?

_____
_____
_____
_____

Are we called to do what He did?

_____

Now, let's look at some of the other things Jesus was called to do and determine if we have been called to do the same.

Read Isaiah 61:1-3

This scripture, through prophecy, perfectly describes the mission of Christ in the earth. If this were His mission, should it not be ours? Are we to bind up the brokenhearted or proclaim the favor of the Lord? Are we to proclaim freedom to captives? Yes, of course we are! This is how we display His splendor. We display His splendor by doing the things that He did. We are His hands extended, His voice speaking comfort, His truth bringing freedom. We are a planting of the Lord in this garden He created for mankind.

Read Matthew 15:13

Read Jeremiah 17:8

The difference between the two plantings is glaringly apparent. The bottom line is this: When all that we do finds roots in Him and is done to show His glory, we grow from strength to strength, displaying His splendor to the world. When all we do is rooted in our own desires and is done to our own glory, we are cut off, having nothing of worth to offer.

As I once again stand before that mirror, deciding if I truly am ready, may the words of King Lemuel ring through my heart, testing it, "Charm is deceptive, and beauty is fleeting; but a woman who fears the Lord is to be praised" (Proverbs 31:30) and planted!

Do you know with all certainty that you are a planting of the Lord?

_____

What would your response be to His question, "Are you ready?"

_____
_____
_____
_____

Will you do anything differently in response to today's lesson? If so, what?

_____
_____
_____
_____

Questions or comments concerning today's lesson:

Day 3

Perfect Wisdom

"She speaks with wisdom, and faithful instruction is on her tongue."

Proverbs 31:26

What a beautiful observation of the virtuous woman! Most of us have brief moments where we actually say the right thing, give the appropriate godly response; the Word of God springing to our lips before our opinions take over and tumble mindlessly forth, birthed by emotion instead of wisdom.

I am sure you have all experienced situations where your words truly brought comfort and direction to someone who badly needed it. You saw the light bulb go on in their eyes, or dried tears as the conviction of the Holy Spirit flowed through your simple words.

I usually walk away from those instances with three words flowing from my spirit, "Thank you, Lord." For, you see, I know that there is nothing good in me. I know that when I am left to my own devices I will inevitably fail. I know that it is only by His grace and His anointing that I am able to offer any wisdom or any comfort.

In that daunting moment when there seems to be no appropriate words, He is there, speaking truth, giving solace, touching wounded hearts with His healing. The most amazing thing about it? He is using these human forms, in all of their weakness, to accomplish these awesome things in the earth.

Let's look today at how we may learn to walk in the wisdom of God, making every effort to have His mind in all situations.

Read James 1:5

What does the Word say about those who lack wisdom?

_____
_____
_____
_____

James tells us very clearly that God's wisdom is ours for the asking. With this in mind, let's turn to a very important passage of scripture that will explain more about the wisdom that is from God. I want you to take your time reading the following text. Read it until it sinks in and you begin to understand what is really being said. If possible, read it in a couple of different translations. The Amplified Bible gives a particularly enlightening depiction of this "perfect wisdom."

Read I Corinthians 2:6-16 and answer the following questions.

What does verse 6 tell us that this wisdom *is not*?

___

What has been revealed to us (verses 9, 10)?

___

Who may discern the thoughts of God (verse 11)?

___

Let's look for a moment at verses 12 and 13 and make some practical applications. Verse 12 tells us that we have been given the Spirit of God so that we may understand what God has freely given us. It goes on to say in verse 13 that we are to share the spiritual truths (concerning scripture) that God has revealed to us.

Our conversation is not to be full of human wisdom, opinions, vain conceits and lots of "me's and I's," but should offer the truth of the Word.

A friend shared a story with me one day as we were talking. She had been going through a difficult time and needed counsel, so she contacted a woman in whom she had great confidence, spiritually. She shared her concerns with this friend and then asked her, "Well, what do you think I should do?" The spiritually mature woman replied, "I am not going to tell you what I think you should do, but I can tell you what the Word says about your situation." What a wonderful, Christ-like response!

When given the opportunity to offer our opinions, too often we jump in headfirst and then later think, "Hmm, wonder what the Word says about that?" Sometimes we do not even consider the Word at all. Our flesh may often give the easy, kind, non-rebuking answer, to keep from rocking the boat or causing someone to be upset with us. This is not what being a brother or sister in Christ is all about.

Read Ephesians 4:25

Does this scripture imply that we are to be cruel and mean in our intent? No. Not at all!

Look a little further (to v. 29). What type of truth are we to speak? Fill in the blanks.

"Let no_____ proceed out of your mouth, but that which is _____ to the use of_____ that it may minister_____ unto the hearers."

Truth operating by grace, given through inspiration of the Holy Spirit of God, is the divine way of living, speaking, walking in the wisdom of God. All of the wisdom we could ever possibly need is found within the Holy Scriptures. Whatever your situation, whatever your crisis or question, your answers are within your grasp. As we learned earlier from the book of James, wisdom is ours for the asking, and after gaining wisdom we will begin to speak wisely.

Wisdom, we are told, is not silent. Proverbs 1:20, 21 tell us:

> *"Wisdom calls aloud in the street, she raises her voice in the public squares; at the head of the noisy street she cries out, in the gates of the city she makes her speech:"*

Am I telling you to cry out in the streets? Only if that is what the Spirit of God leads you to do. I am telling you that there is great need of wisdom in this world, and when it is discovered that you are wise, through Christ, people will be drawn to you. You will have *The Answer* for those who are seeking truth. You will be sought out for counsel and in those times, you must boldly proclaim what the Word of God says. You must never compromise the Truth and Wisdom of God! In order to keep it pure and unadulterated, you have to know the Word. Otherwise, your opinions will be mixed in with Truth, and only pure truth brings wisdom.

Offering yourself to another is an act of kindness for the moment; offering the Word is an act of love that truly transforms the life of the recipient.

That, my friend, is wisdom.

Do you believe that you are currently walking in God's wisdom? Please explain your answer.

_____
_____
_____
_____

If not, what, if anything, do you feel that you should do to correct this situation?

_____
_____
_____
_____

Is there someone in your life with whom you have a relationship that consistently tells you the Truth no matter what?

_____
_____
_____
_____

Do you consistently speak the Truth to others as well as yourself?

_____
_____
_____
_____

Which of the scriptures studied today meant the most to you? Why?

_____
_____
_____
_____

Questions or comments concerning today's lesson:

Day 4

Perfect Mercy

"Blessed are the merciful for they shall be shown mercy."

Matthew 5:7

It is almost impossible to discuss mercy without discussing grace. We have already talked about grace on Day 1 of this week, but we looked at it more from the personal perspective. In today's lesson we will talk about the grace and mercy of God as they go hand in hand to *influence our walk with Christ.*

Vine's Expository Dictionary puts it like this: "*Grace* describes God's attitude toward the lawbreaker and the rebel; *Mercy* is His attitude toward those who are in distress."

Vine's goes on to express the thought that grace must always go before mercy based on the assumption that only the forgiven may be blessed with mercy. While that may be true in some sense, I am struck by the image of our precious Savior standing on the hillside overlooking Jerusalem and weeping for His people, the same ones who had rejected Him, calling Him a heretic. I am reminded of His cry. To this ear, it is a merciful cry, tempered with the thought of future justice. It is God's heart crying out in love, while the righteousness that defines Him decrees what must be done.

Read Matthew 23:37-39

Do you sense the pain in Jesus' words? I can almost hear Him saying, 'Don't you understand how much I love you and how much I want to protect you? I have longed to hold you close to me that you may know my love for you.' To me, this is mercy. Compassion feels the pain of another. It is heart pity for the suffering of others. We cry out for God's mercy every day. We have great need of His understanding, for we are sinful and fail. In this failure we are wounded. His mercy comes and restores us. Mercy is the gift of a loving God.

Webster defines mercy as "The power to forgive or spare from full punishment." This type of mercy is found in Christ's interaction with the woman caught in adultery (John 8:4-7). Yes, that definitely sounds like my Father. He has all power in heaven and earth and He has chosen to love me, daily extending great mercy.

Read Hebrews 4:14-16 and answer the following questions.

Why is He especially equipped to show us mercy?

_____
_____
_____
_____

Why do you believe it is called the "throne of grace?"
_____
_____
_____
_____

What do we go to the throne of grace to receive?
_____
_____
_____
_____

If we take what we have already learned concerning grace and mercy, and apply it to this scripture, we can see His beauty more clearly. Our Savior, Jesus Christ, experienced all manner of temptation while on the earth so that He would be able to understand our human frailty. While He Himself knew no sin in the temptation, He is touched by what we go through when we are tempted. His merciful nature is moved by our frustration, pain and disappointment when we fail the tests placed before us. He moves in and begins to speak truth to us (just as we discussed in yesterday's lesson), and shows us the way out of our suffering.

Psalm 85:10 (KJV) states "Mercy and truth are met together…"

We are moved to repentance by the mercy that He shows when we fail. He then moves in grace and forgives the trespasses and sin that we have fallen into, or more accurately, that we have chosen to walk in.

Mercy and grace come together to expunge the dark marks of sin from the human hearts He has placed within us. Our Spirit man then rejoices in the wonderful deliverance from sin's oppression.

Now that we have taken a glimpse into God's merciful response to us, let's look at what our response should be to those around us. Notice I did not say to those we like, but to all we come in contact with.

We have already taken a look at Matthew 5: 7. Now turn to James 2:12, 13. Fill in the blanks below.

"Speak and act as those_____ by the law that gives freedom, because_____ without _____ will be shown to anyone who has not been _____. _____ triumphs over judgment."

Read Colossians 3:12-14

I love the way this verse reads in the King James translation of the Bible.

> *"Put on therefore, as the elect of God, holy and beloved, bowels of mercies, kindness, humbleness of mind, meekness, longsuffering; forbearing one another, and forgiving one another, if any man have a quarrel against any: even as Christ forgave you; so also do ye."*

"Bowels of mercies." One definition of bowel, given by Webster is "the deepest inward parts." This tells me that mercy is supposed to be an intricate part of who we are. Mercy should not have to be worked up or forced. It should be a part of our nature because the "Father of Mercies" is our Father. As His children, we should bear His likeness. Just as I can look at my oldest son and see the image of his father etched upon every line of his face, so should we resemble our Father of Mercy. (If you want to see reference to God as the Father of Mercy, grab a King James Bible and look at II Corinthians 1:3). Our character should be a shadow of His, our personality a reflection of Him.

Psalm 145:8, 9 (KJV) is one of my favorite passages in the entire Bible. It so beautifully depicts the Father of Mercy that I have come to know.

> *"The Lord is gracious and full of compassion; slow to anger, and of great mercy. The Lord is good to all: and His tender mercies are over all His works."*

What a wonderful God we serve! At this very moment my heart is so full I can hardly contain my tears. He is so good! He makes every day of my life worth living. When I arise in the morning, I will call Him blessed. When I close my eyes to slumber, I will call Him blessed. His name shall be on my lips, His Word hidden in my heart. All of my days are given into His hand and I trust Him with all of my heart. Why? Because He is "gracious and full of compassion; slow to anger and of great mercy."(Joel 2:13)

Gracious Father, make me more like You!

Do you better understand the difference between grace and mercy? If so, explain the difference.

_____
_____
_____
_____

Can you think of a particular instance when His mercy drew you to repentance?

_____
_____
_____
_____

To whom do you need to extend grace and mercy?

_____
_____
_____
_____

Questions or comments concerning today's lesson:

Day 5

Perfect Love

"Love never fails."

I Corinthians 13:8

"Love is patient, love is kind. It does not envy, it does not boast, it is not proud. It is not rude, it is not self-seeking, it is not easily angered, it keeps no record of wrongs. Love does not delight in evil but rejoices with the truth. It always protects, always trusts, always hopes, always perseveres. Love never fails."

I Corinthians 13:4-8

Every time I read the words I am reminded of how wide the chasm is between God's definition of love and my own. If I were to give you my thoughts on love, I am sure there would be mention of heartache and passion, romance and adventure. There would have to be extreme emotional upheaval, because, as we all know, there is no controlling the heart (heavy sarcasm). After all, we cannot help whom we love.

Or can we?

Love, in human terms, requires temper and feelings, heart and soul, tears and laughter, jealousy and competition. Love, in God's terms, requires only one thing - a decision. This decision is what we are going to be looking at during today's lesson. Loving someone is not about warm fuzzies or heart palpitations, although those can be really nice. Loving someone is about seeing them as God sees them, frailties and all, and choosing to extend the heart of God toward them through your actions and demeanor. Loving is all about being conformed into the image of Christ.

Let's break down a couple of these characteristics, shall we?

"Love is patient…"

Patience: The ability to put up with annoyance, misfortune, pain or delay, without complaint or loss of temper.

Turn to II Timothy 2:24 (KJV) and fill in the following blanks.

"The _____ of the _____ must not _____; but be _____ unto _____ men, apt to _____, _____."

I hope the word "apt" jumped out at you as you were completing the verse above. Apt means to have a natural tendency or inclination. The more we stay in the Word of God, the more our natural tendencies change. Where we used to be impatient, cross and without understanding, we become patient, amiable and understanding. As He opens our eyes to the truth of our situation, we are able to extend grace, just as grace has been extended to us. Impatience is steeped in pride, which the Lord hates (see Proverbs 8:13). Impatience says to those around us, 'I am worthy of more than you are offering. I should not have to wait, or continue to deal with this, because I deserve better.' Oh, how our flesh loves to be pampered and get its way at a moment's notice. Our flesh does not like having to wait on anything or anyone.

You may be thinking, "You just don't know what I have to put up with." That is true, I do not. But God knows. He knew before time began, yet He still inspired these words to be written, "Love is patient." While our flesh will revolt, our Spirit, is well able to wait – with patience. Remember;

"They that wait upon the Lord shall renew their strength."

Isaiah 40:31

Do you want just one more reason to be patient?

Look at Psalm 40:1-3

My God hears the cry of those who wait patiently for Him.

"Love is kind…"

Kind: gentle, tender and good. Showing or based on gentleness and consideration.

Read Ephesians 4:32

"…just as in Christ God forgave you."

Just as. If you look at this closely, you will see that we are to be kind, *just as* God is kind to us because of Christ. It is not because we deserve it that God shows us mercy; it is because of Jesus and the sacrifice He made. *Just as* God is kind because of Christ and in spite of our state, so must we be kind in spite of the state of the person and because of Christ's sacrifice for us. Again, as stated in the beginning of today's lesson, we have to make a decision to do what is pleasing in the sight of God. Showing kindness to another when your flesh wants to do the exact opposite is choosing to walk controlled by the spirit, which will always produce life, both for you and for those around you. God is love. Love is kind. To be changed into His image, we must portray kindness, for He is kind.

"It does not envy…"

Envy: a feeling of discontent or jealousy with regard to another's advantages or possessions.

Read Proverbs 14:30

Be happy when those around you prosper. If your brother or sister has more than you, do not covet what they have. Do not make light of all of the blessings you have received, by wanting what your neighbor has. Be grateful to God for all He has done. A thankful heart is a heart that God will continue to bless.

When we envy others, we are basically saying to our Father, "You have not done enough. I want more!" Let us never be ungrateful and greedy. May we always be found extolling the great blessings of the Lord. For truly He is a great God who

> *"Opens His hands and satisfies the desires of every living thing."*
>
> Psalm 145:16

"It does not boast…"

Boast: to speak with exaggeration and pride, especially about oneself, someone, or something connected with oneself.

Read Ephesians 2:8-10

It is not about you. It is not about me. It is about Him. If we are ever tempted to think more highly of ourselves than we ought, we should keep in mind that it is only by His grace that we are not on a direct pathway to hell. Blunt, but perspective-shaping. Our good deeds cannot save us, nor can our good name. Money is irrelevant, as is talent or fame. We have nothing with which to redeem ourselves, save Him. When I am left to my own devices, trust me, I am nothing to boast about. However, in Him, and of Him, I do freely boast. Singing His praises is always in order. My boasting should always be of His goodness, never to build myself up or to cause others to feel less than adequate. It is only His grace that enables me to accomplish anything in this demanding, selfish flesh of mine.

There is so much about love that we do not understand. We all desire to experience it. We look for it, plan it, write about it, sing about it and even paint it upon canvas for the world to ooh and aah over. What we cannot do is define it in human terms. What we must do is make a decision to do and be the things that denote love to this world, as described in I Corinthians 13.

Every day we must decide to be patient when we feel our temper begin to flare. We must show kindness when someone has been unkind to us. We must delight in the good fortune of others and sing the praises of a Creator who is beyond all comprehension. And you know the wonderful thing about all of this? We get a chance to start over every day. If you behaved badly toward a sister yesterday, today you can apologize and receive mercy. If you were unkind last week, you can show kindness today.

Love is renewable. It never runs out. We are changed from glory to glory as we grow in this decision to love. We may feel like we have failed in our endeavor to portray the love of Christ, but keep in mind love never fails. His love always accomplishes what our human efforts cannot.

Questions or comments concerning today's lesson:

Poured out

Here I am again, Sweet Lord,
My vessel parched and dry,
Moistened only by the tears,
I have no strength to cry.

My head too heavy Lord to lift,
My feet too sore to stand,
Back fair bent with burdens great,
Holding forth an empty hand.

Rivers of Your life I seek,
Oil enough to fill,
This vessel, then to drench the cups,
Of all who thirst and will.

Springs to wash away the draught,
Fresh rain from Your throne,
Dew so sweet, please wash these feet,
That I may kiss Your own.

Wash away all trace of dust,
Wells of water shout,
Come closer still, Your vessel fill,
For I must be poured out!

Class Notes:

Week Two

I Wish Someone Had Told Me What it Means to be Faithful

"I will betroth you to me forever; I will betroth you in righteousness and justice, in love and compassion. I will betroth you in faithfulness, and you will know the Lord."

Hosea 2:19, 20

Day 1
Faithfulness of God

Day 2
Faithfulness of God

Day 3
Faithfulness of God

Day 4
Faithfulness to Commitments

Day 5
Faithfulness in Marriage

Are you a faithful person? Do you do what you say you are going to do? Can the people you deal with on a daily basis trust you? What kind of reputation do you have concerning faithfulness? Do you care what kind of picture you project concerning this area of your life? Oh, I hope so! Not for your sake, but for the sake of Christ. Our God is a faithful God. He is honest, full of integrity, honorable, truthful and just. We are called to be like Him, so we may check our progress by applying those characteristics to our own lives to see if we are improving or regressing. When others speak of you are they able to apply these characteristics to their description of you? Are you a man or woman of your word? God is calling you to be just that. The old westerns used the phrase "a man's word is his bond." By giving someone your word, you were bound by that word. Handshakes were contracts because men walked in integrity, upholding their word. Times may have changed, but you know what? God's standard has not. We should be men and women of our word, according to His Word.

Day 1

Faithfulness of God

"Know therefore that the Lord your God is God; He is THE faithful God…"

Deuteronomy 7:9

"I am with you and will watch over you wherever you go and I will bring you back to this land. I will not leave you until I have done what I promised you."

Genesis 28:15

Faithful. Someone who is reliable, who can be counted on to do what He says He will do. Oh, I love that! In a world of uncertainties and ifs we find an absolute, a faithful God. If we could merely grasp this one truth from the Word of God our lives would be absolutely revolutionized. For if He is faithful to do all He has promised, then we are healed, filled, set apart, blessed in our coming in and our going out, sheltered and forgiven. We are in the palm of His hand and no one can snatch us out. When we begin to see God as faithful to His Word, we begin to see how different our lives should be.

Today we will lay the foundation for the rest of the week's study. We will look at the absolute faithfulness of Jehovah God.

Read Deuteronomy 7:7-10.

To whom is the Lord speaking in this passage? (You may have to read back a bit if you are not familiar with the timeline of Deuteronomy.)

_____
_____
_____
_____

Why did the Lord choose the Children of Israel?

_____
_____
_____
_____

Write verse 9 in the space below.

_____
_____
_____

Has God entered into a covenant with you? Notice I did not say have you entered into a covenant with God. W.E. Vine provides a wonderful exposition of covenant that I must share with you. He states, "In contradistinction to the English word "covenant" (lit., "a coming together"), which signifies a mutual undertaking between two parties or more, each binding himself to fulfill obligation, it (the covenant), mostly signifies an obligation undertaken by a single person. For instance, in Galatians 3:17 it is used as an alternative to "promise." God enjoined upon Abraham the rite of circumcision, but His promise to Abraham, here called a "covenant," was not conditional upon the observance of circumcision, though a penalty attached to its nonobservance."

Are you getting the picture? God has made a covenant with us based upon Him, not us. The Word tells us in Hebrews 6:13 that when God made His promise to Abraham "He swore by Himself, since there was none greater for Him to swear by." "Faithful and True" swore by Himself that He would remain faithful. How long? This is where it gets really cool (My son would really be making fun of me right now for using that word)!

Turn to Psalm 105 and read verses 8-10.

He remembers His covenant how long?

_____
_____
_____
_____

For how many generations?

_____
_____
_____
_____

And what kind of covenant is it?

_____
_____
_____
_____

Words like *forever*, and *everlasting*; oh, bliss! He will be here forever just being faithful to me and loving me. How selfish that must sound to the world, but how very precious it sounds to this spirit sojourner.

Let's look at just a couple more things to tie a bow on this. For starters, let's be practical and put this concept in human terms, since we with our finite minds, have trouble comprehending eternity. Return to Deuteronomy 7:9 for a moment. It states that God is

"Keeping His covenant of love to a thousand generations of those who love Him…"

Let's see, a generation is considered to be 40 years (give or take); 40 x 1,000 = 40,000 years. Taking into account that these words were written less than 4,000 years ago, we still have approximately 36,000 years remaining on just that one promise. So, in the year 38,000 AD… You get the idea. You want to see the exciting part now? That was the Old Covenant. We have a new and improved one!

Turn to Hebrews 12:24.

Jesus is referred to as what in this passage?

_____
_____
_____
_____

Now read Hebrews 13:20. Fill in the blanks.

"May the God of _____ who through the _____ of the _____ Covenant, brought back from the dead Our Lord Jesus, that great Shepherd of the sheep, equip you with _____, for doing _____, and may He work in us what is _____ to Him through _____, to whom be the glory forever and ever. Amen."

God's covenant with man is a covenant of love. He promised to love us for eternity. There was never any question as to whether or not He would love us; the question was how He would redeem us. He had to make a way for us since He had made a covenant to love us, and He could have no part of sin. The sacrifice of bulls and rams atoned for the sin of man – covered it, just as God slew the animal to make skin coverings for Adam and Eve after they had sinned. However, the covering was only for a short period – until the person sinned again (which for most of us would be a same day occurrence). Therefore, constant sacrifice was being made for constant sin.

But God, in His infinite wisdom, compelled by His amazing love had already set in motion the ultimate sacrifice; a sacrifice that would atone for the sin of men once and for all. Through this sacrifice a new covenant would be established, a covenant of reconciliation and relationship. There would no longer be mere remission of sin; there would be access to almighty God through the sacrifice. What could formerly be done by an appointed few would now be promised to all -

communication with God through a Great High Priest, the Sacrificial Lamb, Jesus Christ. A new covenant was set in place when Jesus died on the cross. We now could be filled and re-filled with the Spirit of God. His blood cleansed us from sin as nothing else could have. Knowing the gift that had been given drew us to Him as sheep and goats never could. Love was demonstrated on the cross, establishing a new covenant based not upon works, but upon grace.

Romans 8:2 states it perfectly:

> *"For what the law was powerless to do in that it was weakened by the sinful nature, God did by sending His own son in the likeness of sinful man to be a sin offering."*

The old covenant of a loving faithful God was not abolished on the cross, but was fulfilled. For, once again, man could walk with His God in the cool of the day and fellowship with Him as he had in the garden. Because of the covenant set in place by the blood of Jesus Christ, we will be His children for eternity. He has "sworn by Himself for there is none greater." He is faithful to His promises.

We will talk more of faithfulness tomorrow.

Having completed today's lesson, how do you see God's commitment to you?

_____
_____
_____
_____

Having seen perfect faithfulness displayed, what do you think of your own level of faithfulness toward God?

_____
_____
_____
_____

Write a prayer asking God to help you become more like Him in the area of faithfulness.

_____
_____
_____
_____

Questions or comments concerning today's lesson:

Day 2

Faithfulness of God

Yes, this is the same title as yesterday. Would you like to know why? I will tell you. The story of God's faithfulness could not be written upon all the pages the world has to offer, so I feel quite certain we can find fresh, insightful material for another couple of days. Today, I would like to look at why we are so drawn by the faithfulness of God. In a society that likes to teach there are no moral absolutes, we find great comfort in a God who draws the line and says "This far, and no further." Just as children take comfort from knowing their boundaries, we too, take comfort inside the protective boundaries of a limitless God. Sounds like a contradiction, doesn't it? Well, it isn't. Today we will see how the faithfulness of God gives us the freedom to be everything we were created to be. Why? Because,

> *"He Who began a good work in you, will be faithful to complete it."*
>
> Philippians 1:6

My daughter, Kaitlen, was almost six years old. There was so much she was just beginning to understand. Questions would spring to her beautiful little lips every 30 seconds or so. She wanted to know everything right now, and was not pacified by the words, "just because I said so." But there were times (many times) that was the answer she got from me. The reason she often got that answer was because she had more than likely asked that same question *several* times before, and thought if she continued to ask, my answer might eventually change and become one that she liked. It usually went something like this;

"Why do I have to clean up my room?"
"Because your room is your responsibility. You need to be able to actually find your clothes and shoes instead of guessing where they are."
"But why?"
"Because your life is much easier when you know where your things are, and when you take care of all of your things they last much longer."
"But I will be too old to play with my things if they last that long."
"Kaitlen, if you outgrow your things we will be able to give them to someone else if they are in good condition."
"But, momma, I don't want to give my things away!"
"Kaitlen, just go and clean your room please."
"Why, mama?"
"Because I said so!"

Have you ever had this conversation (or a form thereof) with your child? Or even more to the point, have you ever had this conversation with God? "Lord, why do I have to…?" We continue to beseech God about something when He has already given us the answer. Why? Because we are hoping He will change His mind and give us something easier to do. The irony of it is that, His way will always be the absolute best way. Why do we think for one minute that we might possibly see a better angle to the whole situation? Without fail, the things we want to talk God out of most are the things that cause our flesh to be humbled. This flesh screams, cries, moans, groans, begs and pleads, "Please, God, anything but *that*!" Usually the *"that"* means death to the flesh and life to the spirit. It is just difficult to see the life when looking through eyes of flesh. Paul seemed to address this very issue in Ephesians.

Read Ephesians 1:18.

What do you suppose Paul meant by *the eyes of your heart*?

_____

_____

_____

I believe Paul was asking that our spiritual eyes be opened to see what God is doing instead of merely looking with human eyes that see the circumstances. I believe if we can begin to see the faithfulness of God with the eyes of our heart, we will pass through doors that have held us captive for years. For if we really believe He will be true to His Word, we have a wealth of promises we have yet to claim. We will begin to act on what He has told us, begin to seek out His Word to see what we might be missing. When we believe that God will complete the work He has begun in us, we want to know what that work is. If He will truly never leave me, then I want to be careful what it is I am doing when He is around. If God will never forsake me, then why am I listening to the voice of the accuser saying, "Oh, you've done it now, He'll never take you back this time!"

Let's take a few minutes and look at some of the promises of God. When you read the following verses, insert your name in the appropriate places. For example Psalm 91:7 "A thousand may fall at MY side, ten thousand at MY right hand, but it will not come near ME." Get the picture? Make the Word personal. It is personal. It is your life we are talking about here!

Read Psalm 91:1-15.

Pray and ask the Lord to show you areas in your life that may be lacking in faithfulness. List those areas below and recommit yourself to God in these areas.

_____

_____

_____

Tomorrow we will be talking about how God is faithful to expose the lies of the enemy. Get a head start on tomorrow's lesson by asking the Lord, through prayer, to make you very aware of deception in your walk with Him. Ask Him to reveal any area where the enemy may be voicing his opinion instead of God's absolute truth. Be in prayer about tomorrow's lesson.

Questions or comments concerning today's lesson:

Day 3

God's Faithfulness, Continued

Let's begin today's lesson with the truth of the Word. Let's look at some of God's promises. We do not want to miss anything the Lord may have for us.

Psalm 145:13b

"…The Lord is _____ to all His promises, and _____ toward all He has made."

Psalm 145:8, 9

"The Lord is _____ and _____, slow to _____ and rich in _____. The Lord is good to _____; He has compassion on _____ He has made."

Isaiah 53:5

"…by His wounds we are_____."

Luke 12:32

"Do not be _____, little flock, for your Father has been pleased to give you _____."

Psalm 119:165

"Great _____ have they who _____, and nothing can make them _____."

Protection, love, grace, compassion, healing and peace are just a few of the promised favors of God. And, because He is faithful to His Word, all of these belong to those who are called His own. Are you one of His chosen children? If you have accepted Him as your personal Savior, you are. If you are saved, and are walking around in fear, your inheritance has been stolen from you. If you are holding something against your brother and harboring bitterness inside of you, you are being robbed. Healing is yours because God has promised it. Peace is yours simply because He said so. He is *The Faithful God*. There is no other that is faithful as He is faithful. All of His promises are "yes and amen."

Name it and claim it? No. Believe and receive.

What is the difference? *Name it and claim it* infers that we decide what we want, then we claim it in the name of Jesus and we have it. Believing and receiving, on the other hand, is based on our belief in a faithful God, our belief in a multi-faceted omnipotent creator. We believe in a God who formed the universe and who maintains complete control over it. This effects what we "claim."

To put it very lightly, as Bill Cosby used to say concerning his father's form of to-the-point discipline "I brought you into this world, and I can take you out of it." All power concerning life and death, have been given into the hands of this faithful God we serve. No, He is not waiting for you to do something wrong so He can take you out; He is waiting for you to see the Right so He can bring you in.

I want to share with you an experience of my own that seems to fit perfectly here.

Sometime ago I was having a particularly trying day. I just could not get anything right. I began to lament my lot in life concerning my calling in Christ. I felt like ("felt" should be a real red flag) I was just never going to get it together. I kept feeling (there is that word again) like a big hand was getting ready to swat me like a fly. In my mind I could just see God shaking His head, a displeased look upon His face. To be honest, I had walked around with that image of God for so long that I thought it to be true. I felt a constant displeasure from Him. Because of that, I walked in a constant state of defeat. I gave up easily, and made excuses for my behavior. After all, if I was not going to be able to do it well enough to please Him anyway, I may as well just give up now, right?

I began to talk to myself as I cleaned the kitchen. (Yes, I do talk to myself on occasion, and I also clean my kitchen – though one I do more frequently that the other!) I remember saying, "God, I am never going to be good enough for You. It is just too hard! I cannot do everything it takes to make you happy. I just can't." You know, it is funny, but you can never really *just* talk to "yourself," for He is always listening.

As soon as the words left my mouth, I heard Him speak so clearly to my heart; "Barbie, if you never do another thing in your life, I am pleased with you. My love does not change based on your performance. I loved you before you even loved me." Then I heard Him say what would become a revolutionary truth for me for me; "All of the things I ask you to do are for your benefit, not my own. Laws have been set in motion on the earth and I am trying to teach you how to operate best within its system. You salvation was by grace alone, not works. Your works are to your benefit, not mine."

I stood in my kitchen thinking about what I had just heard. Could it be true? Was God really pleased with me just because He loved me? How could that be? What about all of the hellfire and brimstone? What about Dante's Inferno? You know, man hanging over flames? Could I really be acceptable to God just as I was?

For an instant my mind was carried back to a time when one of my sons was much younger. The family was getting dressed up for a family portrait, everyone hurrying around trying to find what they needed to be just perfect. I walked into my son's room to find him sitting on the bed, head bowed as he stared at his "dress clothes" on the floor in front of him.

"Why aren't you getting ready?" I asked as I sat down beside him.

"I don't know," came the quiet reply.

"You need to get ready, honey, it's almost time for our appointment."

"Momma," his little voice broke, "I don't want to have my picture made."

"Why, sweetheart?" I asked, expecting the 'I-don't-want-to-put-on-a-tie' speech.

"Because I'm ugly."

Tears sprang to my eyes as I wrapped my arms around that child. I told him exactly what my heart knew to be truth.

"Oh, baby, you are absolutely beautiful. There is no one in this world like you."

You see I knew from experience that this world could be cruel beyond words. The enemy of our soul's peace roams about like a roaring lion seeking whom he may devour. He had sent cruel words to me before, just as he sent them to my son now. His desire is to undermine our faith in God by keeping us focused on our fleshly limitations. Satan will point out every flaw you have and then replay the tape repeatedly in your mind. You begin to focus on the lies and the truth takes a backseat. You become convinced that you are unlovable and unacceptable and you are being devoured by his animosity toward you.

My son had taken to heart the cruelty of the enemy. I rocked him in my arms and comforted him the best way I knew. I told him the truth of who he was. Smart. Funny. Witty. Tender. Beloved. Beautiful. Soon, the truth began to sink in. When time came for the portrait, his beautiful smile transformed the simple family photograph into a work of Heart.

Truth is transforming. It changes us. The lies of the enemy change us too. That is why we must pray with Paul that we have a

> "spirit of wisdom and revelation, so that we may know him better."

We must pray that

> "the eyes of our heart be enlightened in order that we may know the hope to which he has called us."

I fell to my knees on my kitchen floor that day when the Lord spoke to my heart about my being pleasing to Him just as I was. I repented for my lack of faith and for my lack of knowledge of the scripture. For if I had known the Word, I would have known that I am created in the image of God. I am His child and I am acceptable to Him. I am pleasing to Him.

In His faithfulness, He will not change His opinion of me. He knows me through and through and still finds me beautiful. He will be faithful to me always. I never have to wonder what He thinks about me. I know He loves me dearly. How do I know? Because He said so!

How do you think God really feels about you?

___

Upon what do you base your opinion?

___

Have you ever believed a lie? If so, what was its effect upon you?

___

What happened when you discovered the truth?

___

Questions or comments concerning today's lesson:

Day 4

Faithfulness to Commitments

"In the same way, their wives are to be women worthy of respect, not malicious talkers but temperate and trustworthy in all things."

1 Timothy 3:11

A few years ago my friend, Mary, and I began teaching a women's class entitled "Sister to Sister." The objective of the class was to address everyday issues, applying the Word of God to the unique situations that women must face in their daily walk with Christ. The class began with a bang! The two of us were so excited about what God was going to do through that class. Our dreams were big, our focus intense.

We studied and prepared our lessons, putting all that we had into the teaching of the class, and for a while, things went great. Attendance of the class was high, as was the commitment level. Ladies would show up, Bible in hand, notepad pages turning, ready to hear what the Lord might have for them that particular week. It was such a rush to me. I would sit down at my computer, all of my concordances, dictionaries, commentaries and Bibles by my side, and ask God to show me what He wanted me to share that week, and He would *show up*! I mean His Word would begin to tumble through my mind, verses I had forgotten I had known; insight I could have only gained through Him. Before I knew what had happened, hours had passed and right in front of me on the screen was a teaching only He could have orchestrated.

It was such a wonderful time for me. I was learning what it meant to submit to Him in the area of study. I was experiencing for the first time what it really meant to be a teacher of the Word. It was an important time of growth for me. I loved what I was doing.

"So, what," you ask, "has this to do with faithfulness?"

I am getting to that. You have heard the expression "Into every life a little rain must fall?" Well, it began to sprinkle. Summertime was coming on and attendance began to decline. Children's ballgames, family commitments, general familiarity, began to take its toll. What used to be a thriving class became a small discussion group. The small group was good, but it was not the vision I had cast. Discouragement nipped at my heels and lethargy made a nest within my heart. I stopped studying quite so hard, began putting less and less time into preparation and missed numerous appointments with my Heavenly Father. What had once been a source of great joy became a drain on my resources. Why? Because I was not fulfilling what God had called me to do.

When He put it within my heart to teach the class, He did not say, "Study to show yourself approved…as long as you have the largest class possible." He had told me to study to show myself approved unto God. I had given up because of circumstances. I had become unfaithful to the call of Christ in my life.

Proverbs 3:12 tells us that those whom the Lord loves He rebukes and disciplines. He must love me so much, because He sure did discipline me. I felt like such a failure. No, He did not make me feel that way, but He did not rush in and force me to quit wallowing in self-pity either. How could something that started out so well, end in such a mess? I mean, by the time the class ended, Mary and I were really the only ones left. It was so sad.

Do you want to know what is even sadder? I went on to do the same thing to a couple more classes. I would begin them with the best of intentions, only to become discouraged and give up when things did not go as planned. I was riding the "double-minded roller coaster" of unfaithful service.

Finally, one day, after a particularly disheartening class, the Lord spoke gently to my spirit. "How long will you be satisfied by less? How long will you give little and receive little? When will you become faithful over little, so I can make you ruler over much?"

I began to cry. I was so unhappy with where I was spiritually. I walked in constant defeat because I was just too lazy to do what He had called me to do. He would instruct me through His Word, and I would walk away from it, doing what was easiest to my flesh, and death to my spirit man. I was an unfaithful servant. I did not do what I said I would do when He called me. You know, those on-your-knees-promise-I-will-if-you-will moments.

I had told my Lord that I would be a student of His Word and then teach all that He had shown me. In fact, I had become a student for much too short a time, and attempted to teach what I myself did not practice. It was such a struggle, and in the end, I had given up the fight when what I should have done was to dig into the Word and grow in faithfulness. I should have begun to do what I knew to do.

You cannot ask a child in kindergarten to write a book report. You must first teach the child the alphabet and allow time for perfection. You must show them what an "A" looks like, what it sounds like, and then help them to write it for themselves. They can then put it together with the other letters they have learned, and make a complete sentence.

In the same way, you cannot have someone teaching a class who may know what sections of the Word look and sound like, but does not have a grasp of the whole picture. I had all of the head knowledge gained through years of Christianity (knew my ABC's), but had not the faithfulness to walk it out (make sensible sentences). I was a very inconsistent, unreliable servant. Trust me; this is not what God's body needs. We need preachers and teachers who are faithful to do all that the Lord has called them to do, and all that their calling requires.

These failures in my own life started me on a journey toward faithfulness. It was not something taught by my father, for though he tried, he was ultimately unable to remain faithful in many areas of his life. My mother, by contrast, was as faithful a person as one could ever hope to know. I must have taken after my father, for it was his traits I most often displayed. Then, as the Lord began to show me that I must be faithful if I were going to go one step further with Him, I had to dig in my heels and force this lazy body to conform to the image of His spirit within me. What was my first step? Learning to finish what I started.

Below are a few search-your-heart questions. Ponder them then answer in the space provided.

Have you committed yourself to something that you now wish you had not? If so, what?

___

Did you pray before committing to this particular thing or area? Did you get a clear answer from the Father as to whether or not you were to be a part of this?

___

Have you ever just given up on something, leaving a mess for someone else to clean up? If yes, explain.

___

What kind of representation of Christ do you feel that you are in the area of faithfulness?

___

If you were the only "Jesus" that a person might meet in their lifetime, would they think of Him as faithful?

___

Do you finish what you start or are there more unfinished projects at your house than completed ones?
_____
_____
_____

Do you feel that it is important for you to be a woman/man of your word? Why?
_____
_____
_____

Who was the absolute best example of faithfulness in your life (excluding Christ)? Why?
_____
_____
_____

What characteristics did they display that caused you to name them as your example? What were they like?
_____
_____
_____

I would like you to find three scriptures that directly relate to God's will concerning faithfulness, and write them on the lines provided.
_____
_____
_____
_____
_____
_____
_____
_____

Questions or comments concerning today's lesson:

Day 5

Faithfulness in Marriage

"Marriage should be honored by all, and the marriage bed kept pure…"

Hebrews 13:4

What comes to your mind when you consider faithfulness in marriage? If you are like most, your immediate thought is to the physical. No one likes to consider that their mate could possibly be unfaithful in this area of the marriage union. The vows that we made to one another to "Keep thee only unto him or her" were commitments and promises that we know are never to be broken. Physical infidelity destroys homes, breaks hearts, shakes foundations, ruins self-esteem, obliterates trust and can scar the soul of all parties involved. I say it scars the soul, because this is the seat of your emotional stability. When your security is shaken in this manner, it is very easy to lose touch with yourself - to feel the need to re-evaluate whom and what you thought you were. What you believed to be true about the person you chose as your life mate is suddenly no longer true, and you can begin to doubt all of your judgments, especially about members of the opposite sex.

Infidelity in marriage is nothing short of devastating to all parties involved. Looking merely at the physical impact, saving the spiritual for just a moment, the partner who cheats loses all credibility and respect, not to mention the fact that they often lose a family they still profess to love. The offended partner must confront anger, betrayal, self-recrimination, self-doubt, bitterness, shame and other damaging emotional baggage.

Then, as if devastating two lives were not enough, there are the innocent children - those trusting hearts whose very existence revolves around this family unit. Their examples in life, their mother and father have all of a sudden taken away their stability – both physical and emotional. It is emotional because they experience the same sense of abandonment and betrayal that the offended adult feels, often leading to stresses and self-recrimination they could otherwise have avoided. It is physical, because all too often mothers are left to support children on their own. The financial strain is so very demanding. The lifestyle of the mom often changes dramatically, as does the child's. Nothing is ever the same in a household afflicted by unfaithfulness. Unless…

"…with the Lord there is mercy, and with Him is full redemption."

Psalm 130:7

Trying to put a marriage back together after one partner has been unfaithful physically is one of the hardest things on earth to do. But, do you know what? My God excels at making the hardest things seem like the easiest. It is all about turning to Him as your ultimate healer. Letting Him become the true love of your life. Only through complete and total dependence on Christ can broken vows become renewed, trust rebuilt and lives reestablished.

I strongly suggest Christian counsel to any couple struggling with this problem in marriage. Do not give up and do not give in. If you want your marriage to survive, it truly can. Not with just one person trying to keep it together, but with both working full-time to connect, heal, forgive, nurture, communicate and respond in love toward one another. Moreover, remember, repentance is imperative. To repent is to turn completely away from the direction you were heading and go in the complete opposite direction. The offender must make sure that they have first received the forgiveness of Jehovah God, and then they must seek the forgiveness of their mate. Unless a heart has turned from sin, there will be no progress or healing. Adultery is a physical offense, but its origin is completely spiritual. Sin issues and your relationship with God must be settled before ever trying to reestablish your marital relationship. A "flirt" must come to realize there is no such thing as an "innocent flirtation."

Read Proverbs 21:8.

What does it say about your conduct?

_____
_____
_____
_____

We must not play with temptation. If you are "just that way," just be that way with your spouse. Feel the need to joke, tease, play and flirt with your eyes? Your spouse should be the one to enjoy that playful side of your personality. Want some spice in your love life? Great! I am sure your mate would too. Talk to one another about your needs, desires, thoughts and fantasies. You are in a covenant relationship with this person for the rest of your life.

Everything you will experience physically in the years to come will be with this person. If you are having a fantasy you cannot share with him/her, you are allowing your mind to dwell in places it should not be. Ask God to show you how to walk before Him in this area of your life.

Too often sex is seen as dirty or forbidden. Coming to realize that God intended for a husband and wife to take great pleasure from their physical union frees us from inhibitions and needless embarrassment. This knowledge allows us to fulfill our fantasies with our mate, creating a "safety net" of sorts from temptation in the sexual arena. Many marriages would be greatly strengthened by a *consistent*, strong, creative love life.

I highlighted *consistent* because it is a vitally important description of a healthy sexual relationship. Needs return frequently, and should be met in the same manner.

I have a girlfriend who explained to me that she and her husband had gotten out of the "habit" of consistent lovemaking. I was so surprised, because to be honest about it, I did not think it was possible for both partners to get out of the "habit." Most often, one partner, usually the wife, loses interest and the other partner must either give up or fight constantly with their physical urges. This is such a dangerous place to be. The mind of the unfulfilled mate can become a target of fiery darts of lust and temptation.

> *"The husband should fulfill his marital duty to his wife, and likewise the wife to her husband. The wife's body does not belong to her alone but also to her husband. In the same way, a husband's body does not belong to him alone, but also to his wife. Do not deprive each other except by mutual consent and for a time, so that you may devote yourselves to prayer. Then come together again so that Satan will not tempt you because of your lack of self control."*
>
> I Corinthians 7:3-5

I once knew a woman who wrote on her calendar each time she and her husband made love. Did she do this because she was trying to get pregnant? No, she did this so she could ration her husband. If he wanted to make love and she was not in the mood, she simply pulled out the calendar and said, "Look, last Thursday…" It would be funny if it were not so appalling! How hurtful that must have been. Ladies if you walked up to your husband and wanted to kiss him and he pulled out his planner and said, "Sorry, kissed you Tuesday," how would that make your feel? Angry? Unwanted? Sad? How often would you subject yourself to that before you simply quit trying? I would venture a guess that it would not take too long.

What happened to the woman with the calendar? Her two children grew up without a father. He eventually gave up. Was he right in doing what he did? Absolutely not! Could it have been different? Absolutely!

What about my friend and her husband who had gotten out of the habit of making love? They did something about it. They began to do what Gary Smalley calls "creating love." They made a conscious decision to come together to create love in their marriage. For a while, they drove me crazy acting like a couple of newlyweds! They went everywhere together; started dating again. They looked for ways to surprise one another. It truly changed their marriage. It was very sweet, and quite inspirational. My point? You can do something about the state of your marriage. Prayer is vital. Communication is mandatory. Nevertheless, actions speak louder than words. Walk in your decision to love your mate.

Today's lesson went in a different direction that I had intended. However, knowing that I have given this to God, I feel confident that this is where we were meant to go. Please prayerfully consider the words you have read today. Take stock of your current relationship with your spouse. Those of you who are not married, take today's lesson to heart so that you may never fall into these particular traps should you marry in the future. Remember, it is not about sex, it is about taking every opportunity to "create love" in your marriage. Your bodies were designed to give and receive pleasure within the physical union of marriage. It is more than okay to make love. You are "fearfully and wonderfully made" in such a manner that you may offer comfort, passion, tenderness, pleasure and love to your spouse. You have God's permission, even His blessing, to enjoy this part of your marriage. Now, go forward in the blessing of the Lord.

Special Assignment: Read Song of Solomon three nights in a row.

Has today's discussion made you uncomfortable? If so, why?

_____
_____
_____
_____

Do you feel that your mate is pleased with this area of your marriage?

_____
_____
_____
_____

Do you believe that God would have you do anything differently concerning the physical aspect of your marriage?

_____
_____
_____
_____

Do you really believe that marital sex is a good thing? Do you feel released to be creative and passionate?

_____
_____
_____
_____

Write a prayer asking God to free you in this area of your life. Submit your mind (and all of its preconceived notions concerning sex) to Him. Ask Him to renew your mind in this area.

_____
_____
_____
_____

Questions or comments concerning today's lesson:

Beloved

Come, Oh Come, sweet Bridegroom dear,
My lips whisper your name.
Merest touch from gentle hand,
This love is yours to claim.

Long, Oh long, this aching heart,
At Blessed's feet now fall.
Sweetest voice, speak unto me,
His words, sweeter than all.

Look, Oh Look, upon Him now,
Fairest Lover see.
Turn your cheek into His palm,
His love does flow through thee.

Hold, Oh Hold, the strongest arms,
Rest safely troubled head.
For He has come, The Lovely One.
Be gone now, troubled dread.

Heart, Oh Heart, consumed by flame,
Passions fire refined.
For at last, I am Beloved's
And He is truly mine.

Class Notes:

Week Three

I Wish Someone Had Told Me I Am Fearfully and Wonderfully Made

"I praise you because I am fearfully and wonderfully made; Your works are wonderful, I know that full well."

Psalm 139:14

Day 1
In The Beginning

Day 2
The Weight of the World

Day 3
Losing Yourself

Day 4
What About Me?

Day 5
Better Things

Do you ever feel like just giving up? Do you wake up in the morning wanting to do what is right, but find yourself doing the exact opposite by the end of the day? Do you see other Christians who seem to have it all together, then wonder if you will ever be like them? Do you feel like you stumble more than you walk? Are you constantly harassed by thoughts of failure and feel like you are never going to get the hang of this whole Christian thing, though you have been saved for a very long time?

If this sounds like you, you have opened the right book. Not only have you opened the right book, you are talking to the right person. I have been there (sometimes still go there), and I have longed for something more from my walk with Christ. I am in search of the perfect Christian life, but as yet have not found it. What I have found are people just like you and me, doing their best to be found pleasing to a God who is already pleased with them. I have found fellow sojourners who wish they could "measure up," when they are already loved beyond measure. What I have found is that there are no perfect Christians. There are only imperfect children of God depending upon the mercies and grace of a loving Father. For all of us truly have sinned and fallen short of the glory of God, but… "There is a redeemer…"

Day 1

In the Beginning

"For You created my inmost being; You knit me together in my mother's womb; I praise You because I am fearfully and wonderfully made; Your works are wonderful, I know that full well."

Psalm 139:13, 14

The 139th Psalm has always been a favorite of mine. When I really need to know how He feels about me, I turn to the 139th Psalm. Though there are countless passages that speak of His love for me, I am somehow drawn back to this passage. Why? I think it is because it gives such a detailed depiction of His involvement with my day-to-day life. It tells me that He is watching over me at all times. I used to find it quite unsettling to think that he was watching me all of the time. My discomfort at the thought surely stemmed from my lack of obedience to His commands – my sinful nature that had a tendency to dominate at the time.

When I was a teenager, my mother used to tell me, "While you are on this date, I just want you to remember that Jesus is riding in the back seat of the car with you." Man, what a bummer (Like Jesus did not have anything better to do than go to the movies with me). It truly was not that I was planning to do anything bad; it was just that if I had wanted that kind of company I would have asked my mom to go. In those days, I saw any type of guardianship as a lack of trust. If my mom would not let me go out with a group of friends, then it was obviously a lack of trust. If Jesus had to go to the movies with me, He must not trust me either. What I failed to comprehend was that in both my mother's and my Savior's case, trust was not the issue. Love was.

I am not intimating that the whole "Jesus in the backseat" thing was true, but I do know that in every moment of my life, He has been present. He has been watching over me and caring for me from the very beginning.

Read Psalm 139 and fill in the blanks below.

"O Lord, you have _____ me and you _____ me. (v.1)

You know when I _____ and when I _____; you perceive my _____ from afar. You discern my _____ and my _____; you are familiar with _____ my ways. Before a _____ is on my _____ you know it _____, O Lord."

This scripture used to scare me. There are still moments when it causes me pause. Which is a good thing. However, for the most part, 99.9% of the time (okay, 96.5% of the time), it brings such comfort to my life. It tells me that I am not as alone as I may feel. It tells me that I am not going through anything all by myself. It tells me that there is always a shoulder waiting for my tears, always-strong arms to pick me up when I fall.

How do I get that from this scripture? This passage seems to me to be a perfect picture of a parent who loves his child. This parent wants to know where his child is at all times. This parent wants to know what is going on in the mind of his child. This parent listens well and understands what his child is saying. This parent is always there for the child, and if this parent is there, you know that they are picking the child up and dusting them off when they fall. This ever-present parent is in the full-time business of caring for their child. You have such a parent. And this is the beginning.

We have all heard stories about, seen television programs concerning, and may even know someone who has been adopted and is looking for their birth parents. In most cases, the child feels a need to "connect" with that birth parent because of a profound need to know "who they are." Even though the child has, in most cases, been raised by loving, adoptive parents, there are still some questions they feel the need to answer for themselves; "Where did I come from?" "What is my real father like?" "Did they want me?" They know there are answers out there and find it virtually impossible to get a sense of peace and release until those questions have been settled in their minds.

In the same manner, God has placed within each person a heart that searches for answers. We all want to know where we came from – our point of origin, so to speak.

Read Genesis 1 and 2.

Answer the following question:

"What is my real Father like?"

_____
_____
_____
_____

Read Psalm 145:8,9,13-19.

"Did they want me?"

_____
_____
_____
_____

Read John 16: 27, John 3:16, John 15:16.

In order to know who we are, it is essential that we know where we came from. No, I am not talking about your earthly parents, though they have been your primary source of self-recognition and character development. You may have the absolute best parents on earth. However, if you fail to recognize yourself as a spirit – an eternal being, created and placed on this earth by a God who loves you more than life itself, then you are not fully aware of how "fearfully and wonderfully made" you truly are. If you base your worth on the flesh, then no matter how beautiful or intelligent or talented you are, there will always be someone better.

If you base your personal worth on the spirit man inside of you, your worth becomes limitless. Your capacity to love through the spirit makes you an extension of your Creator. You offer this world something it searches for, longs for and needs more than anything else, a glimpse of a Savior who loved them enough to die for them. You are hope to a world that has given up. You are light to darkened hearts. You are truth to a generation lost in deception. You were created in the image of God. You are a vessel that houses the Holy Spirit of God. How much more do you need to know about yourself?

He loves you. No one can ever take you out of His hand. You are His child.

The question is never whether or not He will love you, but whether you will love Him?

Have you accepted Christ as your personal Savior? Do you know in your heart that He loves you as His precious child? _____

Finding your identity in Christ always begins with Him, not you. With this in mind, write a short prayer asking God to reveal more of Himself to you, so that you may know your Father better.

_____
_____
_____
_____
_____
_____
_____
_____
_____
_____
_____
_____
_____

Questions or comments concerning today's lesson:

I Need You So

Will you hold me when other arms are closed?
Will you speak kind words of love...
When my heart aches from bruises inflicted by harshness?
Will you look at me and see beauty...
When other eyes fail to see anything remotely pretty?
Oh Father, I need You so....

Will your eyes smile in pleasure when they glance my way?
Will you overlook the small failures...
When others seem to hold them under a magnifying glass?
Will your gentle rain of compassion cover me...
When others sit down to judge?
Oh Father, I need You so....

Will You talk with me when others have no time?
Will You listen to and take pleasure in my songs and poetry?
Will You understand what I feel when I write?
Will You hold me...
When the tears will not cease no matter what I do?
Oh Father, I need You so...

Will You find my thoughts provoking,
My conversation stimulating...
When others wear a mask of boredom?
Will You hide me away...
When I am hurting so bad that I cannot face the world for this day?
Will You be my best friend and companion...
When I am utterly alone?
Oh Father, I need You so...

Will You be everything to me?
Will You fill the gaping holes in this heart?
Will You exchange my wickedness for Your goodness?

Oh Father, I need You so...

Day 2

The Weight of the World

"Come to me all you who are weary and burdened and I will give you rest."

Matthew 11:28

Who you were yesterday is not the same person you will be today. That can be a good thing or a bad thing depending upon if you liked yourself yesterday or not. For some of us, the thought of change seems like a wonderful, bright promise somewhere on the horizon - a chance to do something different, break out of the routine, crawl out of the rut. For others, the mere thought of change starts a reaction in their physical body that overwhelms them. Their throats constrict, their stomachs churn, and their thoughts take off on a mad dash, trying to figure out how to keep things "just the way they are!"

Whatever category you may fall into, I would like to establish here and now: *Change is coming – Ready or Not.*

Read Ecclesiastes 3:1-8, preferably in the Amplified Bible.

The seasons of our life are varied and diverse. Yesterday you may have laughed until your sides ached, only to find that today you are unable to stem the flow of tears. You may have danced in church Sunday morning, only to find that you could barely lift you head from the pillow on Monday. Change comes in Spirit, soul and body on a daily basis. Our soul is changed by emotion, our body changed by circumstance, and our spirit by spirit. The area we tend to change most often is soul (what we think and feel). Our body runs a close second, and our spirit, unfortunately third. Why?

Our focus is on each of these areas is proportionate to its level of importance to us. We tend to focus most on how we feel about things (Soul). We then look at everything around us to see if we have been validated in feeling the way we do. Do our circumstances warrant our feelings (Body)? Then, after exhausting our resources concerning feeling and circumstance, we turn to God (Spirit). We are, in essence, saying, "I will handle this myself, and if by some chance what I am doing does not work, I will see if God can help me."

Our first choice should always be spirit. Our spirit man should be in a state of constant change. You know, the whole "from glory to glory" thing. If you are satisfied with where you are spiritually at this moment, you are in trouble. I did not say if you were pleased with where you are, I said satisfied, which means: to put an end to a craving or appetite. If you are satisfied where you are, you are no longer "craving" or going after the deeper things of God. What do I mean by deeper? I just meant *more*. Every step you take with God will take you deeper. Satisfaction takes away your need for change, and we all must change in the spirit.

Read Matthew 18:3.

What are we told we must do?

_____
_____
_____
_____

Become like a little child. Innocent. Trusting. Loving. Tender. Open. I do not know about you, but if becoming like a child is my goal, there are going to have to be some major changes in this girl's life! This realization brings me to the reason for the title of today's lesson, "The Weight of the World." For it is this world that has changed us from innocent to guilty, from trusting to fearing, from tender to hard, and from open to hidden. The things that happen to us in our lives here on earth change us.

I was 11 years old when my body began to change from that of a little girl to the fully developed body of a young woman. By the time I was 13, I was 5' 9" and my body had outrun my mind by a long shot. I thought that because I had the body of a woman, I must surely be one. I considered myself vastly more mature than the other girls my age and started to run around with an older crowd. During that time I developed my first "I'll die if he doesn't notice me" crush. This guy was handsome and talented, had a great car, ran with all the cool people…and was six years older than I was. One night a group of us (my mom would never have agreed to let me date anyone – especially someone that much older) went to the bowling alley to goof off. I thought I was just so cool, hanging out with the older, more popular kids.

I strutted (yes, I truly did!) around the scorekeeper, who just happened to be *The Guy* I had the crush on, and said something that I'm sure I thought would be clever/enticing. I batted my eyes and giggled in that special way, as I picked up my bowling ball. During my back swing I heard his voice call to me over the din of loud music and the laughter of all of my "friends," "You know Barbie, you're great from the neck down."

The ball slipped from my fingers and plummeted toward the gutter. I pasted a smile upon my lips and turned back to my friends, laughing with them. Nothing had changed on the outside. I was still the cut up, still the smart mouth, still the one who laughed the loudest. But on the inside, everything had changed. The confidence had left, the laughter had been silenced and my identity had been altered. What happened? I had been handed a "weight of the world."

This is what Satan does best. He deals you a blow through someone you trust, and your trusting heart becomes guarded. He sends a disparaging, judgmental look through the eyes of someone whose opinion you respect, and the confidence you once had goes fleeing before you. He wounds us with daggers held by the hands of friends, for they are the most painful and most unexpected. The hate-filled words of a stranger do not have the impact that the harsh words of a friend have.

We place our confidence in human vessels and are repeatedly disappointed and hurt. Does this mean that they are bad people? No, they are human, and were never intended to be the recipient of all of our confidence and trust. They are people carrying weights of their own, often just looking for a place to unload. They are changing, just like you and I. Coping, adjusting, shifting, and yes, unloading.

So, what do you do? If everything around you is changing and there is no stability in the earth, where do you turn? When you are fed up with the weights, where do you go to lay yours down? Look for the strongest, most stable, completely unchanging rock, and just drop them!

I know such a Rock…

"…who does not _____ like shifting shadows."

James 1:17

"I the Lord do not _____…"

Malachi 3:6

He was good to you yesterday and He will be good to you today. He had shoulders strong enough to carry your "weights" yesterday. They are strong enough today.

Read 1 Samuel 15:29. Write the verse on the lines below.

_____
_____
_____
_____

In one sentence, paraphrase Hebrews 13:8.

_____
_____
_____
_____

Yes, everything is changing. You most of all. God is constantly at work in our lives prompting us to draw closer to Him. In order to do that (draw closer to Him), we have to shed some of the stuff in our arms. In order to put our arms around Him, they need to be open – not clutching onto things.

Our pursuit of "stuff" will change us. We will become driven, selfish, tired, self-centered, and carnal. Our pursuit of God will change us too. We will become more childlike every time we call Him Father. We become more innocent every time He washes away a sin. We become less guarded and more open every time we trust Him with our hearts. We become less weighted by this world, when we choose to let Him bear our burdens. Who you are today is not who you were yesterday, or who you will be tomorrow. You will change. The choice of *how* is up to you.

Read Deuteronomy 30:11-20

What, if anything, will you change today?

___
___
___
___

Questions or comments concerning today's lesson:

Day 3

Losing Yourself

Okay, now that we have spent the last two days finding ourselves, let's get rid of us. Finding out who you are is a good thing, but it is not going to help you out a great deal in the long run. Finding out who He is - now that is a different story.

As I sit here trying to put my thoughts together for today's lesson, I find that I cannot get rid of a picture that keeps running through my mind. I keep seeing the "horse of a different color" from the movie *The Wizard of Oz*. You know the one. It is yellow one minute, purple the next, then red, or green. That may not be the exact order of the color change, but you get the gist. Why is this on my mind? Because that is rather how I feel about the whole "finding your identity in Christ" business. How you actually find your identity is based largely upon whom you talk to. The horse changes colors from denomination to denomination, from era to era.

Ultimately, your identity in Christ is not what is important. It is Christ Himself, the hope of glory, within us that will shape our identity. More of Him, less of you. More like Him, less like you. Your identity becomes entwined with His. You begin to look and act like Him. Soon, you are found *in Him*, and your identity really does not matter anymore. It is He alone who matters.

We, as the Body of Christ, have, unfortunately, gotten away from the pursuit of knowing Him, and have turned instead to a secular mindset of knowing ourselves. Not a good thing. We can search, and look and dig deep into our psyche and never find the real meaning of life. We look at Him and are saturated with life itself, and the meaning becomes quite clear. But, then again, that has been one of Satan's schemes all along. If He can get our eyes off of God and onto ourselves, then He has stopped our forward progress. We do nothing for the Kingdom when we are consumed with ourselves. That works for Satan! He is quite pleased with that outcome.

If you are tired of looking for the problem deep within yourself you must consider looking outward and upward for your answers. The following are examples of great men of faith struggling with their fleshly side. It may help you to see beyond your failures.

Abraham. Man of faith. Father of the Jewish nation.
"Tell them you're my sister, not my wife."

David. Man after God's own heart.
"Send Uriah to the front lines of battle so that I may have his wife."

Moses. Delivered the people of Israel by the Lord's hand.
"Glancing this way and that, seeing that no one was about, he killed the Egyptian and hid him in the sand."

What is going on here? I am showing you that even the great ones missed it sometimes. I could cite occasion after occasion where people who knew better, did bad things. The biggest reason? Fear. Abraham was afraid that he would be killed if the king wanted his wife, so he told her to lie and say that she was his sister. It was not a total lie, but the intent to deceive was definitely there. David was afraid that Uriah might find out about him and Bathsheba, so he had him sent into a battle guaranteed to kill him. Moses was afraid of being caught and convicted of murder, so he hid the body and fled to the dessert.

We do the same thing; hopefully not the whole burying the body in the sand bit, but definitely the deceiving, not-the-whole-truth part. We pretend that everything is great (deceiving) so that no one will know how weak we really are. Why? Fear. We are afraid that if someone really knew what we were like our whole cover would be blown. We would no longer be Miss Super Christian. That would be the equivalent of death for us socially. After all, they only like you because you are so good, right? I mean, can honesty really be the *best* policy?

Read Proverbs 12:17-22, Zechariah 8:16, 17 and Ephesians 4:15.

What does the Lord delight in?

_____
_____
_____
_____

Is honesty really the best policy? It is His policy. That makes it the best.

Before we all run off thinking we have a license to rip someone to shreds with the truth, look again at Ephesians 4:15. Pay close attention to the "in love" part. Do not correct me with the truth unless you love me. What you perceive to be truth, "Her hair looks really bad," may merely be a fact, not the truth. As our pastor has often said: *Facts change, Truth does not*. My hair may look really bad today, but tomorrow it may look great. The facts will have changed, so I really did not need you to state them to me, and in doing so, ruin my day. The truth would have been Psalm 45:11.

Did you look it up? I know, it is a little over the top. Okay, a lot over the top, but it is truth. It will not change tomorrow, or in a thousand tomorrows. See the difference? The truth heals and brings hope. It corrects, disciplines and rebukes. Why is this so important?

> *"…so that the man of God may be thoroughly equipped unto all good works."*
>
> II Timothy 3:17

That is the power of the truth. It changes us from who we were to whom He created us to be. Okay, here we go. Let's tie this together with the title of today's lesson, "Losing yourself."

Read Roman 12:1-3.

If the truth transforms us…

Transform: to change in condition, nature or character.

And transform means to change…

Change: to remove and replace.

And change means to remove…

Remove: to take away or off.

And remove means to take away…

then we are taking away, or laying down our old identities, in exchange for the truth of Christ. We are "losing ourselves" as we become identified with Him through the truth of the Word. As we see ourselves mirrored in the truth of the Word, we begin to see those things that are spiritually unattractive – that's a nice way of saying "the ugliness of our sinful nature"- and we want to lose that part of us; to give it up; have it removed. A kind of spiritual plastic surgery begins to take place as the "two-edged sword" of the Word begins to cut away at the flesh, leaving less of us, more of Him. We are much more "spiritually attractive" after this process takes place! We may have some recovery time, getting rid of the flesh can be quite painful, but our Great Physician has a marvelous bedside manner and will have us up and running in no time, if we follow His instructions to the letter.

It is God's desire that His children become well acquainted with Him. Paul expressed it beautifully in the third chapter of Ephesians. He was praying for people he cared deeply about, and this was his prayer:

> *"I pray that out of His glorious riches He may strengthen you with power through His Spirit in your inner being, so that Christ may dwell in your hearts through faith. And I pray that you, being rooted and established in love, may have power, together with all the saints, to grasp how wide and long and high and deep is the love of Christ, and to know this love that surpasses knowledge – that you may be filled to the measure of all the fullness of God."*
>
> Ephesians 3:16-19

Filled with the fullness of God. It is hard to fill a vessel that is already full. You have to make room if you want to be filled. If you take ice cold, clear sparkling water and pour it into a glass half filled with dirt, what do you get? Doesn't sound very appealing does it? Take that same water; pour it into a shiny clean glass. Better? You bet! Same thing applies to your spirit. Want the fresh, clean, pure life of the Lord? Do not pour it into a vessel full of you. Selah.

As you have studied today's lesson, has there been something that has consistently come to mind, that you know you need to "lose" for the cause of knowing Him more intimately?

_____
_____
_____
_____

What was the last thing you felt the Lord leading you to change about your life? Have you done it?
___
___
___
___

Questions or comments concerning today's lesson:

Day 4

What About Me?

"Do nothing out of selfish ambition or vain conceit, but in humility, consider others better than yourselves. Each of you should look not only to your own interests, but also to the interest of others."

Philippians 2:3, 4

I can just imagine it now. All of the nosy people out there are saying "See, I told you it's okay for me to see to the interests of those around me!" Many a good woman (and man) has fallen into the trap of sticking their noses into business not their own. I have been guilty of it more than once. It is amazing how we can find a scripture to fit anything we want. Twist just a little, embellish a bit, and "being your brother's keeper" can give you license to really make a mess out of someone else's life. What a shame. I feel reasonably sure that most of us are having a hard enough time just managing our own affairs without adding to them the job of judging Sally's. But, if you preface your concern for someone else with the "without selfish ambition or vain conceit" part of the scripture, a different picture begins to take shape.

Read Philippians 2 and answer the following questions.

Verse 1 asks if you have four things. List those four things in the space provided.

1. _____
2. _____
3. _____
4. _____

Our attitude should be the same as that of Christ Jesus.

He took on the nature of _____. (v.7)

He _____ Himself and became _____ to death…"(v.8)

We are told to:

Do _____ without _____ or _____. (v.14)

When was the last time we had that in operation in our lives?

Can you imagine never grumbling or complaining again in your lifetime? Hard to imagine, but look at the reward…

> *"…so that you may become blameless and pure, children of God in a crooked and depraved generation, in which you shine like stars in the universe…"*
>
> Philippians 2:15

I grew up in a very small town in East Tennessee. The children I went to school with in the first grade were the same children I wore a cap and gown with upon my graduation from high school. After being in class with someone for twelve years, you really get to know them. I mean, the football team turned into the basketball team, then into the baseball team. Same athletes, different season. This was an extremely small town! Anyway, in this class there was a pretty, shy, quiet (know it is not me already, huh?) little girl named (believe it or not) Angel. Angel never played a sport, never made the cheerleading squad, never ran in with the *In* crowd. I do not remember her ever wearing anything but demure dresses. During recess, she would swing all by herself or talk with the teachers. She had friends, but she was not like them.

She never seemed to be sad or angry. In all of our years as classmates I saw only one thing that disclosed how Angel was feeling – her smile. Angel smiled from the time she walked into school until the time she left. When you looked at her she smiled, when you spoke to her she smiled and blushed. She was intelligent, congenial and warm. She did not speak ill of anyone or try to bring attention to herself. If she could help you in any way, she happily did so, never asking for anything in return. She was a wonderful, kind person.

There was only one problem with Angel, as good as she was, no one ever really got to know her. She would walk into your world for a moment and bring a ray of sunshine, but she did not invite you back into hers. She gave, but she did not allow you to give back. She could touch you, but you could not touch her.

This is what I see every day in the realm of Christianity. We give. It is easy to give, and we often get recognition for it. However, actually letting someone in is a different story. We see giving as good and benevolent, Christ-like. We see needing as weakness, sin, shortcoming and failure. But, you know what, as much as I liked Angel, she never became a part of my heart.

Perfect people seem to have no need of another. We shut everyone out when we fail to acknowledge that we too have frailties. We make people feel like failures when we appear to have no flaws. We become inaccessible. I might have really connected with Angel if she had come in one day and said, "I'm having a horrible day. My parents do not have a clue who I am." I would have been comforted by the fact that her parents were just like mine, her problems of a similar nature. There might have been a like-mindedness that could have led into relationship. We are missing this connection in the body of Christ. No, I am not talking about grumbling and complaining. We have already established that God is not pleased when we behave in this manner. I am talking about allowing the testimony of your weaknesses to strengthen others and spur them on toward Christ's strength.

If I cannot "humble myself," admitting I am not perfect, then you must keep up your own facade of perfection. Neither of us can receive any help, nor do we find relationships where the compassion of the Holy Spirit may move freely between our two hearts.

This is what I believe Paul was talking about when he spoke of "looking to the interests of others." It is moving beyond our own needs and concerns and caring about others. It is sharing our heart with others so that they, in turn, feel free to share their own. It is all part of becoming the Family of God - learning to care about others more than yourself. I can almost hear some of you saying, "What about me? Who is going to care about me?" Think about it for a moment. If we are all called to care for others more than ourselves, then there are countless people out there more concerned with you than for themselves. While you are thinking about them and praying for them, they are thinking about you and praying for you. It all works out to the advantage of the obedient. It is kind of like someone saying, "You can move this load of bricks alone, or all of these people can help you." Seems like an obvious choice, doesn't it?

Unfortunately, some of us are still opting to move them alone out of the fear that someone may see a flaw if they work too closely alongside us. Brothers and sisters, this ought not to be so.

God's ways will always be higher and better.

Questions or comments concerning today's lesson:

Day 5

Better Things

"And we, who with unveiled faces all reflect the Lord's glory, are being transformed into His likeness with ever-increasing glory, which comes from the Lord, who is the Spirit."

2 Corinthians 3:18

Today I feel compelled to extend hope to His children. I know that some of you are on the verge of giving up. You have said to yourself, 'I just cannot do this anymore; take this anymore.' It is all that you can do to function from day to day because your life has not turned out the way you had planned. But I bring good news, my friend. There is more! You really do get another chance. Your circumstances may not change in this moment but your heart most assuredly can.

Proverbs 13:12 tells us that "Hope deferred makes the heart sick." Therefore, today, whether you are abounding in hope, or deeply lacking it, we are going to take in the hope of the Word and allow it to heal our hearts – to renew that life that makes all the difference in the world.

Write Jeremiah 29:11-13 in the space provided.

_____

_____

_____

_____

Now, take your time, and read the following scriptures. Allow God to speak to your heart as you journey through His Word. When the Holy Spirit is allowed to minister to you as you read, the words on the page become alive and penetrate your heart. If you are in need of hope today, God stands ready to pour it into your spirit, soul and body.

Proverbs 23:18

Psalm 37:37

1 Corinthians 2:9-10

Isaiah 40:28-31

Romans 5:1-5

"...and hope does not disappoint us, because God has poured out His love into our hearts..."

Romans 5:5

I know that my children love me. They must, to put up with a lot of my "stuff." My moods change, and often with that, my mode of discipline: a smart reply from my oldest son, who is very quick-witted, might get a snicker one day, and a *Go-To-Your-Room!* the next. My middle child, the gymnast, may get away with doing a round off in my living room this morning, only to be blasted tomorrow. Is this a good thing? No, but it is a human thing. Many times our reaction to our circumstances is based largely upon what is going on inside of us at the moment. My children may think I am losing it, but I know they never doubt my love for them. Doubt my sanity? Yes. Doubt my love? No. Whatever the circumstances, my love for my children is a constant. It does not change because of their behavior. Nothing changes my love for them. When they are having a hard day and would like to shut me out, that is when I move in closer. When they are struggling, you had better believe I am there!

Do you see where I am going with this? Satan loves to convince God's children that He is going to desert them at the first sign of weak faith. He loves to tell us that we will never measure up, never be good enough. He speaks lies to our minds and tells us we are ignorant, or ugly or flawed in some unique, no-one-else-in-the-world-has-this-problem, way. He taunts and torments until we feel ourselves starting to believe the lies. We draw away from God who loves us because we think we do not deserve that love. Satan has stolen our hope. Satan has convinced us to put a barrier between ourselves and the only hope we have – Christ in us, the hope of glory. Think about it. We feel hopeless, ashamed and unlovable, all because someone who hates us passionately has whispered lies about us.

Tie that together with my analogy of my children. If they are messing up, feeling like a failure, where am I going to be? Parked outside their door just waiting for an invitation to help. If two of my children are doing wonderfully, conquering every obstacle, excelling at everything, and one is really down on themselves, struggling just to make it through the day, where do you think my heart will be?

Read Matthew 18:12-14.

If you are struggling, no matter what the problem may be, He is with you. He has sought you as one lost and is waiting to carry back to safety. You have not strayed too far. He is moved by His great love for you and will reach out to you with most tender compassion. He bought you with a dear price and is unwilling to let you stay where you are. He wants you with Him, now and forever. He has a plan for you – to give you hope and a future. Fall into His arms and allow Him to comfort you as only He can. This is a pivotal moment in your walk with Him. This day you must choose whether you will let Him be the Comforter in your life. In Him is the hope of abundant life here and now, and eternal life to come. He offers all of His resources to you – to heal, restore, comfort and build your faith. Take Him up on His offer. It is the best one you will ever get!

Questions or comments concerning today's lesson:

CLASS NOTES

Week Four

I Wish Someone Had Told Me About Worship

"Let everything that has breath praise the Lord. Praise the Lord."

Psalm 150:6

Day 1
The Exchange

Day 2
It is Just Your Life

Day 3
To Praise Him

Day 4
In The Assembly

Day 5
Just Between You and Me

Beverly would stand in the front row of the small choir, tears pouring down her face, her hands raised to the heavens, her beautiful alto voice carrying across the congregation;

"Oh, for a thousand tongues to sing praises to our king…"

The song modulated, her voice lifting to pour out a pure offering of praise;

"My soul doth magnify the Lord, my soul doth magnify the Lord…"

The tears continued to stream, creating small wet circles at the base of her collar. The choir joined in and we sang from our hearts, telling our Savior how much we loved Him.

Such a beautiful, stirring memory. Lofty praise that lifts us for the moment as we transcend fleshly barriers and enter into praise to our Father. This type of worship is wonderful. There is nothing quite like it. The type of worship we are going to be talking about this week has very little to do with choirs and robes, but everything to do with clean hearts. This week we will talk about a lifestyle of worship - offering ourselves to Him in grateful obedience. We offer ourselves to Him; He pours Himself out for us.

Let the exchange begin.

Day 1

The Exchange

I remember it like it was yesterday. I was eight years old. My daddy walked to the front of his little storefront mission, stepped up onto the rough plank stage, picked up his battered guitar and lifted his blue/gray eyes in search of little brown ones framed by auburn lashes. "Barbie, come up here and let's sing us a song." My feet shuffled beneath my ankle length gown. My head remained bowed as I walked the short distance to where my father stood. He looked down at me as I lifted my eyes to his…and he smiled. The corners of his eyes crinkled in his deep bronze face, and his teeth shone bright and beautiful. He was such a handsome daddy. "You wanna sing Born Again," he asked me as he began to strum the guitar in a rhythm that I recognized as that of one of our "home songs;" you know, the songs you sing when you are just sitting around at home with the family. He faced the congregation and began to sing in his raspy baritone voice; "Satan tried to tell me I just thought I'd got saved…" my little girl voice joined in quietly, but I did not look at the people, I was looking at my daddy. We finished the verse and the next thing I knew, daddy and I were singing loud and clear, "I'm born again, free from sin. I'm happy night and day. It makes me shout, there's no doubt, I know I'm born again."

When the song ended, my father walked me to the edge of the platform, my small hand tucked snuggly within his large square palm. As I stepped from the stage, brown eyes once again met with blue, and in that moment I knew how much my father loved me. Not because I had sang with him when I had been afraid, but just because. Because he was my daddy. We had shared a moment, and in that moment there had been an exchange. As we sang, I caught a glimpse of my father's heart and he had seen into mine.

Almost thirty years later, I am still moved to tears when I think of that moment with my father. I still hear his voice. I still feel his hand holding mine. I still see the crinkles in the corners of his eyes when he smiled.

That smile was just for me. It was mine alone.

It was not about the song, it was about the exchange.

Read Isaiah 61:1-3.

This is a very familiar passage of scripture often used to tell of the Lord's special anointing to minister upon the earth. Today I would like to look at the scripture in a little different context.

About Worship

Please complete the following exchange list:

We Give	He Gives
Captivity	_____
Ashes	_____
Despair	_____
Mourning	_____

It does not seem fair, does it? All of His good for all of our bad. That is only the tip of the iceberg. Look with me at something I found to be quite precious.

Read Isaiah 64:6.

What does it tell us about our righteousness?

_____
_____
_____
_____

Now, turn to Revelations 19:8.

What has taken place?

_____
_____
_____
_____

If you said an exchange had taken place, you are starting to get the picture. In our interactions with Christ, however great or small, something always changes hands. We bring Him little and He makes it much. We bring Him tears, he exchanges them for comfort; we bring questions and He gives us understanding. We bring Him praise; He gives us Himself.

Read Romans 12:1.

What does the scripture tell us to offer?

_____
_____
_____
_____

What kind of act is this?

_____
_____
_____
_____

Okay, so what kind of exchange is this? If you look a little further down in the passage, you will see a couple of things that begin to take place after you have given yourself over to Him as a spiritual act of worship.

Fill in the blanks from v.2 b

"Then you will be able to _____ and approve what God's _____ is – His good, pleasing and _____ _____."

We begin to worship Him in our bodies by transforming our minds with the Word. As our minds are transformed, we begin to hear our flesh less and our spirit more. His voice becomes clearer and more distinct as we offer up the desires of our flesh and exchange them for the desires of the spirit.

Worship is not about vast choirs and countless instruments, though they most definitely bring glory to Him through utilization of our gifts and talents. Worship is about human hearts laid bare all before a loving God. It is about offering our "Born again, free from sin…" with little squeaky voices, pouring forth from pure hearts and having Him think it is the most beautiful thing in the world.

In that moment, if you look very closely, you just may see smile lines appear in the corners of ageless eyes.

About Worship

Questions or comments concerning today's lesson:

Daddy, I Remember...

I remember the way you smelled,
    Of *Old Spice* and hard work

I remember the sound of your voice when you laughed...
    Like dry sunshine, all raspy and warm...
        Your eyes had tiny crinkles in the corners
            From laughing hard, and often

I remember the feel of your hand as it held mine,
    Square, strong, callused and safe...

I remember the way the grass smelled...
    After you mowed it...
        Wearing plaid Bermuda shorts... and dress boots.

I remember the way you looked at Mama,
    Right before you'd sneak up behind her in the kitchen,
        Wrap your arms around her...
            And make her smile a secret smile.

I remember the way you played the guitar,
    While all of us girls laughed
        and danced around your feet.

I remember the first time I sang with you in church,
    "...Born again, free from sin, I'm happy night and day..."

I remember...
All of the good things.
    The wonderful man that you were.
        The lives you touched and changed.
            The souls that were won to my Savior

Because of your love for Him

The way that you smelled,
    Of *Old Spice* and hard work

Daddy,
    I remember...
        And I miss you...

Day 2

It is Just Your Life

"...for they are the kind of worshippers the Father seeks."

John 4:23

What is your personal definition of worship?

_____
_____
_____
_____

You would think with my being a worship leader in my church, that this would be an easy topic for me. You would think that I might easily put the words to page on this one. Well, if that is what you thought, sorry. This is difficult for me. Why? Because I *am* a worship leader. Sounds like a strange answer, I know, but true nonetheless. Because I am intimately involved with this subject, I find it quite difficult to describe. Worship encompasses so many things in my life. It is how I live.

What do I mean? From the time I get up in the morning until I go to bed at night, my heart does worship the Lord. When I choose to do things that I know will please Him, it is an act of worship. When I cry out to Him for help, it is through worship that I do so. When my prayers ascend to Him they are an acknowledgement of His authority over my life – this also, an act of worship. When I speak His Word of Truth, share a testimony of His faithfulness, meet the needs of the poor, care for one who is unlovely, it is an act of worship. And for all of you who may have preconceived ideas about what worship is… yes, you may sing of your love for Him.

Vine's Expository Dictionary tells us,

> *"The worship of God is nowhere defined in Scripture. …it is not confined to praise; broadly it may be defined as the direct acknowledgement to God, of His nature, attributes, ways and claims, whether by the outgoing of the heart in praise and thanksgiving or by deed done in such acknowledgement."*

What does this mean in everyday terminology? You have heard the expression, *actions speak louder than words*? Well, the same applies here. You can sing all of the praise tunes in the world and never enter into actual worship. Worship changes your life, for it acknowledges God as supreme and worthy of absolute devotion. This worship translates into every waking moment of your day and infuses your sleep with songs lifted from the spirit.

I used to think worship was what happened when the fast songs slowed and people raised their hands and began to move to the rhythm of the music. I now realize that worship is what takes place when fast lives slow down and hearts are raised in surrender, as people begin to move to the rhythm of grace.

Worship: *To express reverent honor or devotion to.*

Read Matthew 15:8-20.

Write verses 8 and 9 in the space provided.

_____
_____
_____
_____
_____
_____
_____
_____

Fill in the blanks

(v.18)

The things that come out of the _____ come from the _____, and these make a man _____.

> "...*for out of the overflow of the heart the mouth speaks.*"
>
> Matthew 12:34

How could Jesus say that the people worshipped Him in vain? They were praising Him with their lips, and scripture tells us that out of the abundance of the heart the mouth speaks. Therefore, praise must have been in their hearts for their mouth to speak it out, right?

Look at Matthew 7:21-23.

Many call Him Lord, but God looks beyond the words to the intent of the heart.

> *"And he who searches our hearts knows the mind of the Spirit, because the Spirit intercedes for the saints in accordance with God's will."*
>
> Romans 8:27

For all of those who are looking for that perfect worship experience, let's look at what that really means. In some religious circles, the *perfect* worship would be comprised of lofty music, large choirs, robes and solemn reverence. For others it might be electric guitars, drums and synthesizers. For some it may be absolute silence as the Word is read. There are so many expressions of worship on this planet, there is no way we could possibly put them all down on paper. But do you know what? All of these can be a sweet aroma or rancid stench in the nostrils of God, based upon the hearts of the people offering it up to Him. Vast choirs filled with people who do not acknowledge Him during the week are just another example of Matthew 15:8. For if we sing "He is Lord, He is Lord…" and our lives do not show that to be truth, we have not worshipped Him, we have mocked Him. Strong words, but I believe they are true.

Mock: *to deceive or disappoint.*

In Judges (16:10) Delilah argues with Samson because he has not told her the truth about how he could be bound. She refers to his treatment of her as "mocking." By lying to her, he has belittled not only her intelligence, but also the relationship she perceived them to have. Granted, she was betraying him, but he did not know that at the time. Even in her deceptive state, she was offended by his lies. He had mocked her.

How much more must a Holy God be offended when we stand before Him and lie, calling Him our Lord when our hearts are far from Him. We mock His omnipotent omnipresence when we pretend that He has not seen our hearts, and does not perceive the deceptiveness of our words.

I did not intend to go in this direction today. I fully intended to talk about worship as a lifestyle. I wanted to discuss how everything we do and say is an act of worship. What I had thought to be a teaching on behavior has turned into a moment of searching our hearts. The Lord must be grieved by what we often refer to as worship, when the worship He desires is something else entirely.

Take a few minutes to let God speak to you about how you may submit your heart to Him in true worship. If the Lord should so lead, write a prayer of dedication and commitment to worship Him in "spirit and truth" on the lines below.

_____
_____
_____
_____

_____

Has your definition of worship changed since the beginning of today's lesson? If so, how?

_____
_____
_____
_____

Questions or comments concerning today's lesson:

About Worship

Day 3

To Praise Him

"This is the glory of all His saints."

Psalm 150:9

Read Psalm 149 and 150 (they are short chapters) and complete the following exercise.

What are we supposed to sing to the Lord?

_____
_____
_____
_____

Where are we supposed to sing it?

_____
_____
_____
_____

With what are we supposed to praise Him?

_____
_____
_____
_____

Make music to Him with

_____
_____
_____
_____

What honor are we to rejoice in?

_____
_____
_____
_____

May the _____ be in our mouths.

We are to praise Him for _____ _____ _____ and His _____ _____.

Praise Him with: 1._____, 2._____ 3._____,
4._____, 5._____ 6._____

Let _____ praise the Lord.

David, a man after God's own heart, knew what it meant to praise the Lord.

Read 2 Samuel 6:12 – 22.

I absolutely love this passage of scripture. To me it is about the presence of the Lord coming back into a place that had been without it for so long. The Ark of the Covenant, the tangible sign of God's promise of presence, had to be restored to the city of David, and be brought back by way of praise offerings.

This is so applicable to you and me today. If we have been missing the presence of God in our lives – basically been content to languish without it for a while, out of fear of the changes it might require – it is time to praise Him. If you want something more in your relationship with God, it is time to give more. If you want to experience fullness in the spirit, pour out a praise offering to the Lord. David took everything that was in his heart (think about that in relation to yesterday's lesson) and poured it out with unequalled exuberance before the Lord. He in essence said, "I do not care what anyone thinks. I will rejoice before my God. I will dance with all of my might before the God who deserves all of my mind, soul, heart and strength." He had true worship in his heart and he could not possibly contain it. Remember, "out of the overflow of the heart…"

I believe God was extremely pleased by David's outward show of devotion. I believe He must have felt that same surge of love that we feel when our children do something especially for us. I can almost imagine the smile spreading across His beautiful face as He watched His son show the whole assembly how much he loved Him. When thinking about this moment in time, I cannot help but wonder if perhaps that smile may have turned to tears, as the Father was moved by tender emotion toward the one He loved so much.

The Word of God tells us that He "inhabits the praise of His people." Some translations say that He is "enthroned" upon our praise. It means that He just comes and sits among us when we praise Him. He takes residence in hearts that are given to praising Him. Just think of how He must have flooded David with His presence in those moments as he danced before Him.

In its simplest form, praise is perfect.

>   *"Out of the mouths of babes and sucklings…"*

Psalm 8:2

When was the last time we did *anything* with all of our might? Can we even remember a time when we did anything with all that was in us?

The closest thing I can compare it to would be bringing my children into this world. Giving birth. Talk about full focus! My sons were born without benefit of pain reducing drugs. Every ounce of energy I possessed was spent in those moments preceding their first breath on this planet. I remember thinking that there was no way I could go on any longer. I soon learned that we are capable of far beyond what we think we are. There is an extra *something* inside us that gives us power to complete even the most difficult tasks. We do not call upon it very often. But when the need arises, all of a sudden the strength to accomplish is there.

What do you think that *something* is? As Christians we know it is not some *thing*, but some *One*. The One who,

> *"strengthens and reinforces us with mighty power in the inner man by the Holy Spirit [Himself indwelling your innermost being and personality]."*
>
> Ephesians 3:16 AMP

He is the great equalizer. He makes us ready for anything that may come our way. He is our strength, whether we are bringing a child into this world, or praising Him with all our might. It can only be done effectively when He is involved in the process.

I know, you are saying, "How in the world does she relate childbirth and praising the Lord?" It is a stretch, I know. However, when I thought about the extreme focus David must have placed on worshipping God with all of His might, I could think of very little I do in my life that requires such extreme focus. Anyway, I have complete confidence in the Lord's ability to bring this thing together.

Okay, so how does this compare with praise?

1. Both bring forth life.
2. Both require something from you that you would not normally expend.
3. Both exact a toll, while bringing a thousand-fold return.

When we finally decide that we are going to offer abandoned praise to our God, something will take place in our hearts. A fervent drive will begin to propel us forward into a place that very few go. A place where nothing matters except letting our Savior know how much we love Him, how much we appreciate His goodness, how deeply changed our lives are because of Him. The moment He has our full focus, things begin to happen in the heavens. As we travail (I just looked up the word travail. Did you know it means *as in the pains of childbirth*?) before Him with extraordinary offerings of praise, extraordinary things begin to happen. Life begins to flow through our Spirit and we are renewed and refreshed.

Our praises become wonderful offerings to our Father. He, in turn, comes and dwells among us, filling our lives with the rich fullness of Who He is. Just as we spoke of on day one of this week, a wondrous exchange takes place, and we are never to be the same.

Beauty for ashes.

Strength for fear.

Gladness for mourning.

Peace for despair.

Let everything that has breath praise the Lord! Give thanks unto Him for He is most worthy!

Read I Thessalonians 5:16-18.

In light of the scripture you just read, what do you believe the will of God is concerning you?
_____
_____
_____
_____

Will you put more of yourself into praising Him this week? If so, how?
_____
_____
_____
_____

Questions or comments concerning today's lesson:

Day 4

In the Assembly

"Let them exalt Him in the assembly of the people…"

Psalm 107:32

Today we are going to look at corporate praise and worship. What really happens in the heavens when believers come together in unity for the sole purpose of praising God? What happens to you as an individual when you praise Him in *the assembly of His people*?

Yesterday we studied praise. We looked at several aspects of praise, from dancing to singing, shouting to praying. All are valid forms of praise. I want to take it a little further today; to talk about individual expression coming together in the assembly.

There are as many forms of praise as there are people. Just as each human being is unique in personality, appearance and heart, so is that person's ability to express praise unto God. Some people feel quite comfortable singing softly with the rest of the crowd, while others prefer to be up front with a microphone. Some dancers simply sway within the confines of their pew, while others twirl and leap down the aisle, voluminous skirts floating around their ankles. Some have been gifted to play ivory keys, while others strum stringed instruments. When you bring all of these individuals together and allow them to do "their thing" in honor of their Creator, you have something that is totally beyond our human intellect's ability to comprehend.

The Creative Arts Minister at our church has done much to bring about freshness in our corporate praise and worship. When he first arrived at the church, I think many of us were just a little leery of his *"Want to get more? Give more!"* method of instruction. He had a way of just cutting through all of the garbage and eliminating the whining quota within the praise team. He spoke a lot about consecration (You mean I am going to actually have to give up some carnality?!) and dedication. He began to tell us that we were Levites – a royal priesthood called of God to minister to His people. We thought, "Okay, we can do that. Might be kind of cool." However, somewhere between his teaching, and the actual walking out of giving more to God in way of worship, there lay a fundamental, age-old stumbling block. Written on its side was "But we've never done it this way before!"

Try as we might to embrace this new way of abandoned praise we kept stubbing our toes on this block. If some tried to get rid of the block, others would quickly retrieve it and set it back in its rightful place – which seemed to always be directly in our path.

But do you know what I have found to be true over the years? God will always make a way. God began to bring a wonderfully diverse group of people to our little church. Being located on the fringe of Nashville, a very creative, imaginative city, loaded with performers of all types, did not hurt in the least. As our Arts Pastor began to teach on restoring dance to the body of Christ, through the door came a wonderfully anointed worship dance leader. When he taught of freedom in worship, someone entirely radical for Christ would come in and blow away our perception of acceptable praise. When he told us that praise and worship is not confined to hymnals (I do not think I have seen one of those in our church for a while), the Lord began to give our psalmist's new songs. Step by step (baby steps, in most cases) we began to walk toward Christ with an attitude of, "I'm going to offer You what I have as an act of worship. It may not look like what my friend, husband, wife, etc., is offering, but I give You myself; flaws, idiosyncrasies and all."

What this has birthed in our church has been a miracle at the very least.

God is taking our faithfulness in the small acts of praise, and pouring out blessings I cannot even begin to put on paper. The changes in our people range from subtle to astounding. I absolutely love to watch them. I have a front row view since I am usually on the platform, and I am moved alternately from tears to laughter, to feelings of overwhelming joy and extreme humbleness of heart.

An example:

One woman in particular stands out in my mind. She has struggled intensely to find the freedom that God has for her in Christ Jesus. Coming from an abusive background, she found it difficult to make any outward show of emotion. You could always see a longing behind her eyes. She wanted more of a personal relationship with her Savior, but she felt completely unworthy to ask for what she really wanted.

One night, during a monthly meeting of our Women's Advance, the leaders decided that it would be appropriate to bring the women into the sanctuary, play music conducive to praise and worship, and encourage the women to express their praise of the Father through dance. There was no choreography, no instructional booklet, just a simple request that the women remove their shoes and enter into His presence through the expressive gift of dance.

You can imagine how uncomfortable that was for many of the women. Some, on the other hand, were delighted at the prospect of trying something new. The one of whom I spoke, stopped at the back of the church and simply could not go further. She slid her shoes off and knelt as she watched the others sway, or raise their hands and sing. The whole time that longing lay within her heart, and was visible upon her face. As the night progressed and the women released their hearts to worship in this new way, my fearful sister never found her step.

About a week later I ran into this same woman as she stood outside the sanctuary doors getting ready to enter into the service. Do you know what she was doing? She was removing her shoes! It was during that service that I first saw her "be herself" before the Lord. There was joy on her face as she praised her Precious Father in heaven. She later testified that she had made a decision to never sit back and watch others experience what she herself needed to experience. She had gotten mad enough at the enemy to finally face her fear and *kick her shoes off*.

The leaders had taken a chance and pushed the women just a bit beyond their comfort zone in praise, and look what happened; someone was set free.

Now, please do not misunderstand. I am not saying you have to kick your shoes off in order to praise God. I am not even saying that you have to dance, sing or play an instrument. I am saying that you have to offer God something you would not normally give Him, if you want to receive something more than what you normally receive.

Wayne, our Arts Pastor has been trying to teach us this for quite some time now. Some are taking it to heart, others choose to take him to task for it. Whatever the response may be, at least there is a response. The people are beginning to think about the way they worship God. We are all re-evaluating our offerings of praise, and that is most definitely a good thing. Anytime we take the time to examine our hearts, whatever the reason may be, we have a life-changing opportunity at our fingertips. For when there is a heart exam going on, the true searcher of our heart will be there. He will make it clear to us what our individual sacrifice of praise is. When you know what that is, you have a powerful tool at your disposal. You may then say with King David,

"How good it is to sing praises to our God, how pleasant and fitting to praise Him!"

Psalm 147:1

What is your initial response to today's lesson? (I want your first thoughts here, ladies.)

_____
_____
_____
_____

When was the last time you offered something new to God as an act of worship? What was it?

_____
_____
_____
_____

When was the last time you left your pride behind and humbled yourself in praise of Him?

_____
_____
_____
_____

About Worship

What do you think your sacrifice of praise might be?

_____
_____
_____
_____

Are you willing to make the sacrifice?

_____
_____
_____
_____

Questions or comments concerning today's lesson:

About Worship

Day 5

Just Between You and Me

"He went up on a mountainside by Himself to pray. When evening came, He was there alone."
Matthew 14:23

Today we are going to be searching through a lot of Scripture. Get ready to turn those pages and dig into the Word of God. I believe He has something really special in store for us. Do not miss one piece of this majestic puzzle.

Let's begin.

Read Mark 6:46, 47.

"After _____ them, He _____ _____ on a mountainside to _____."

"He was _____ on land."

Read Luke 6:12.

"One of those days Jesus _____ _____ to a mountainside to _____, and _____ _____ _____ praying to God."

Read Luke 9:28.

"He took _____, _____, and _____ with Him and went up onto a _____ to _____."

Read John 6:15.

"…withdrew again to a mountain by _____."

Please write the following scripture in the space provided.

Matthew 6:9-13

_____
_____
_____
_____
_____

_____
_____
_____
_____
_____
_____

Jesus Christ, the only Begotten Son of God, had to have time alone with the Father. He was perfect in every way, yet He still needed personal, one on one time with God. He was in full-time ministry, in constant contact with Jehovah God, the mightiest man of God to ever walk the earth, yet He made it a habit to withdraw and get alone with God. What did He do in that time? Your initial answer, I am sure, is pray. But, let's look just a little closer.

When I had you write the Lord's Prayer a few moments ago, I hoped that the first lines of the text would literally jump off of the page at you. Particularly the "hallowed be thy name" section of the prayer.

Hallow: *"to make holy or sacred; honor as holy."*

Honor: *"worthy of High Respect"*

Jesus opened His model prayer with an acknowledgment of the holiness of the Father. He offered respect and honor to God with His words. In that simple phrase, He encapsulated the essence of praise and worship – an awesome awareness of the omnipotent grandeur of God.

"Hallowed be thy name."

Matthew 6:9

Did you know that Jesus sang hymns?

Turn to Matthew 26:30.

"When they had _____ a _____, they went out to the Mount of Olives."

At the most difficult point in His life, Jesus sang unto God!

Can you even begin to imagine how beautiful that was to the Father? Maybe the hymn was that of Mary: *"My soul doth magnify the Lord, and my spirit has rejoiced in God, my Savior."* Whatever it may have been, it was nothing short of sacrificial praise. Knowing what awaited Him, He sang of the goodness of the Lord.

Later, in the garden of Gethsemane you will see Him fall with His face to the ground as He prayed. This posture denotes pure and humble worship through physical submission. In His obedience to the will of the Father, Jesus portrayed the most perfect and complete act of worship known to man. He offered worship to His Father before He petitioned Him for anything.

When we think of Jesus, our initial response is probably not, "What a wonderful worshipper!" But, you know what? There never was, never will be, one who loved the Father more. Everything about Jesus' life was an act of worship. He poured himself out as a drink offering for us, as an acknowledgement of the ultimate Deity of God. Christ defined worship with every breath He took, every gesture He made, and every word He spoke.

With this in mind, how much more do you think we, as mere human beings, need to get alone with God and be strengthened by intimate worship? When was the last time you lay prostrate before Him on your living room floor and told Him how magnificent you think He is? When was the last time you could not stop your tears as you crumbled in His presence and bowed your knees in humble reverence? How long has it been since spontaneous praise shook the rafters of your home? When was the last time you basked in His presence?

I do not think I would be mistaken if I ventured a guess that your last "basking" was probably in direct correlation to your last intimate worship experience.

As we said in yesterday's lesson, "Want more from God? Offer Him more of yourself." You can do this in worship like nowhere else. Let Him take you to a new level of intimate worship. Go further into His presence than you have gone before. Get alone with God. Worship Him in spirit and in truth. For this is the worship our Father is seeking.

Questions or comments concerning today's lesson:

CLASS NOTES

Week Five

I Wish Someone Had Told Me Marriage Is Hard Work

"In the Lord, however, woman is not independent of man, nor is man independent of woman. For as woman came from man, so also man is born of woman. But everything comes from God."
I Corinthians 11:11,12

Day 1
A Knight in Shining Armor

Day 2
What Do You Think?

Day 3
Reality and Fantasy

Day 4
The Word on Marriage

Day 5
Putting it all Together

"Marriage", the comedian joked, "is an institution. And who wants to be put in an institution?"

"Take my wife. Please!"

The world has taken something that was ordained of God as holy, and a type and shadow of our relationship with Christ, and has made it trite and trivial. Statistics tell us that more than half of all marriages will fail within the first two to five years. No fault, no guilt, amicable divorces make it very easy for men and women to walk away from vows when things have not gone as planned. But what does God think about all of this? How does He feel about our broken vows? What does He say I should do when I feel like the love has left my marriage? Where do I stand when my husband is not a Christian? Can broken vows be mended? These are just a few of the issues we will discuss in this week's lesson.

If your marriage is perfect, you may skip this week (and call me at home, because I want to know the secret). However, if you find yourself in need of a fuller, more satisfying marriage, come along with me. We are on our way.

Day 1

Knight in Shining Armor

I sat on the sofa, legs tucked underneath me, our one-month-old baby wriggling and cooing beside me, drool sliding off puckered bubbly lips (his, not mine). The guitar, a pawnshop special, twanged as my fingers searched for notes that would have been much easier to find on a piano. The pen and paper lay beside me and I scribbled in between strums. I hummed to myself as I worked, my brow furrowed in concentration, lower lip tugged by my front teeth. Strum. Scribble. Strum. Scribble. My back ached as Baby Aaron decided he did not like the way I played, and began to try to make me quit by digging tiny heels into my side. I sang, erased, sang, erased. Finally, it was done. The ends of my fingers were red and aching from the pressure of the strings, the inside of my lip was chewed to pieces due to my nervous habit of biting it when I concentrate, but it was worth it, because "It" was finally finished.

The house was next. I strapped Aaron into his Snugli, and began to sweep, mop, vacuum and dust with him attached to my chest (Can you tell he was my first child by the fact that I did not make one move without him?).

Now for the meal. I looked into the cabinet. What can one really make out of crackers and sugar? Maybe in the fridge? Yes! Lean Cuisine – we can have a real meal!

I shower, put on perfume, change into my Levi's and one of my good T-shirts. I pad barefooted into the living room to wait on him. I just cannot believe it. One year already. Who would have thought a year ago that I would be in this place today? A wife and new mother to a one-month-old son. Happier than I had ever been.

We lived in a tiny, two-bedroom cottage, had an old blue Ford van, and were absolutely, totally broke. My husband was working construction and consistent paychecks depended upon consistent weather. It did not matter, though, because we did not really need much. Just each other… (Aaah!). That was why, on our first anniversary, I was writing a song for my husband. There was no way we could afford a real gift, so this would be my present to him.

When he came through the door, sweaty and dirty from work, he held out his hand, proud of the flowers he had brought.

"Happy Anniversary, Honey."

"Happy Anniversary," I kissed him.

I placed the wildflowers in a jar and joined him in the living room. "I have a present for you, too!" I told him, as I picked up the old guitar. He sat back and smiled as I began to sing.

> *"I remember so many nights, while sitting on my mother's knee"*
> *"She'd tell me fancy stories about castles and kings,"*
> *"And of ladies in waiting who came to be their queens"*
> *"They lived happily ever after in my dreams"*
>
> *"But I have found in you my knight in shining armor."*
> *"The stories can fade now from my mind."*
> *"'Cause living my life with a knight in shining armor,"*
> *"Is a fairy tail of the sweetest kind."*
>
> *"Now, it may not be a castle we dwell in,"*
> *"But you've made me feel just like a queen."*
> *"And I don't need their diamonds or their silks and satins,"*
> *"I'm happy in my old blue jeans."*
> *"As long as I have known you, my hearts been filled with song,"*
> *"And I know I'm right where I belong."*
>
> *"'Cause I have found in you my knight in shining armor…"*

Seventeen years later:

Much has taken place since that first anniversary. Two more children have arrived on the scene, jobs have come and gone, houses sold and bought, new cities, new schools and new perspectives. Arguments, harsh words, tears and forgiveness have marked our course, as well as laughter, companionship and growth. Things have not been perfect, nor will they ever be, for we are still learning as we go. Throughout all of the changes, however, two things remain constant: God is our source for everything we need, whether spiritual or physical. And Hal is still my knight.

Temples graying, he is still magnificent to me. There have been many times I have shoved him from his horse (taken his position instead of allowing him to do what he is designed to do), and hidden his shield (failed to cover him with prayer and support). I have resented his horse (his mode of provision) and even told the enemy where he was hiding (revealed his weaknesses or flaws to others when I should have spoken his praise in the city gates). Still he is my knight. For you see, my knight has sworn allegiance first, to his Lord and then to me, his bride. Whatever battles may arise, our fealty is to one another. He protects me. He covers me. He provides for me. He still sweeps me away into our own fairytale.

But please remember, even in a fairytale, there is much work to be done between "Once upon a time" and "happily ever after."

Today I want to ask a few questions and stir up some old memories. Pleasant ones, I hope. We are going to take a few minutes and "think on these things."

What attracted you to your husband in the first place? Oh, yes, you can remember! For me it was his long, curly blonde hair and deep tan – superficial huh?

_____
_____
_____

What did he find most attractive about you?

_____
_____
_____

How did the two of you meet?

_____
_____
_____

What was the first thing you remember thinking about him?

_____
_____
_____

Describe your first date with him.

_____
_____
_____
_____
_____

Do you remember the first time he kissed you? How did he make you feel?

_____
_____
_____

Do you remember your first big disagreement?

_____
_____
_____
_____

(If you were able to write more about your first argument than your first kiss, this week's lesson may take more work than we originally thought!)

When was the last time you told your husband that you loved him?

_____
_____
_____
_____

When was the last time you initiated making love? (If you cannot remember, it has been too long!)

_____
_____
_____
_____

What is your idea of "the perfect evening" with your husband? (If it involves fuzzy slippers, flannel and chocolate, remember I said, *with your husband*!)

_____
_____
_____
_____

When was the last time you had an evening like that?

_____
_____
_____
_____

I was going to ask you if you were *happy* in your marriage. I think the more important question would be are you *committed* to your marriage?

_____
_____
_____
_____

If you answered yes to the last question, you have taken the first step toward a fulfilling, healthy marriage. Tomorrow we will talk more about how to arrive at your destination.

Questions or comments concerning today's lesson:

Day 2

What Do You Think?

Yesterday, I purposely took you on a walk down memory lane. I wanted you to remember how you got into this mess in the first place! Just teasing. I wanted you to begin to focus on the time when you fell in love with your mate. Too often we lose sight of what brought us together as we become more and more focused on everything trying to tear us apart.

Let's take a familiar passage of Scripture and apply it to our marriage.

> *Finally, brothers, whatever is true, whatever is noble, whatever is right, whatever is pure, whatever is lovely, whatever is admirable – if anything is excellent or praiseworthy – think about such things. Whatever you have learned or received or heard from me, or seen in me – put it into practice. And the God of peace will be with you.*
>
> Philippians 4:8, 9 (NIV)

"Whatever is true..."

List three positive truths concerning your marriage (i.e. I know my husband loves me).

1. _____
2. _____
3. _____

"Whatever is lovely..."

Can you remember the last compliment you paid your husband? (How many of you just thought, "What about the last time he paid me a compliment?" If you did, ask the Lord to help you focus on your commitment to the relationship, and allow Him to deal with your husband.)

"If there be any praise..."

List three things your husband does that you appreciate, even if you have not mentioned it lately (i.e. Works hard to support the family).

1. _____
2. _____
3. _____

Choose to apply Godly principles to your thought life concerning your marriage. Quit thinking about the bad stuff all of the time. If you are holding onto old hurts and wounds your hands will never be free to embrace the love of your spouse. Release your heart from the torment of animosity and give your husband/wife access to your good emotions. If you constantly think about the bad parts of your marriage, soon that will be all you have.

Many good marriages have been undermined and destroyed because of self-pity and a friend who offers opinions instead of the Word of Truth.

Too often we become focused on the negatives in our marriage instead of the positives. We sit and discuss problems we really have no business discussing with anyone but God. Do I think people need counsel? Yes, of course. What I am talking about though is not a *counseling* session, but a *complaining* session. Let me tell you something that I know to be true. If you talk about the problems all of the time, they become magnified. It is almost as if the problem grows every time you put it out there for discussion. Sisters, there is a big difference between asking for help and looking for sympathy. Be sure that you are doing the former, not the latter. I had to learn this one the hard way.

When I met my husband in 1982, neither of us was serving the Lord. My priorities as well as my lifestyle blatantly portrayed my lack of relationship with Christ, as did his. We married 18 months later. (Sounds funny when you put it together like that!) Having been raised in the church and knowing what I was missing by having shelved my relationship with Christ, I was soon compelled to return to my faith. That was fine with my husband as long as "I just didn't take things too far."

Well, you know how that goes. What is actually "too far" to a charismatic Christian? I began seeking the Lord and trying to draw closer to him. I was attending church every time the doors opened, and I began to (here comes the red flag word) *feel* spiritual. I began trying to deal with all of the things that "hindered my spiritual walk." And I decided that my husband was one of those "things." I let Satan plant thoughts in my mind and I began to toy with them. "I was not serving the Lord when I met him, so I was probably out of the Lord's will when I married him." I began to "think on" something that was not true or noble.

One day after Hal and I had a particularly difficult evening, I went to my friend's house. I just knew she would commiserate with me, and understand, which basically meant I thought she would tell me I was right! The thing I had forgotten was that her husband just happened to be one of the pastors of our church – not a good thing to forget. I sat down at her kitchen table and began to pour out my trials and tribulations. I told her how lonely I felt when I sat behind couples at church (sniff), how hard it was to not have a husband who would pray with me (sniff, sniff). I continued venting until I heard myself say, "I just must have been out of God's will when I married my husband…"

I did not even get a chance to finish my sentence before I heard male footsteps descending with purpose toward the kitchen where we sat. Before I saw him, I heard his voice – yes, the voice of the pastor.

"Wait just a minute, Barbie!" Both of our heads turned as her husband entered the room. "I believe the Lord would say to you "I honor your marriage! Now *you* honor it!"

"But I thought you understood," my voice quivered as I tried to adequately display my turmoil, "I am serving the Lord and my husband is not!" Like that was big shock.

Oh, he understood all right. He saw right through me.

My flesh really wanted to be offended by his intrusion into our conversation, but my spirit leapt within me, recognizing the Truth that the man of God had spoken (Deep calls to deep). The fact that I was not happy at that time did in no way mean that I was out of God's will in having married my husband. It simply meant that we were having a difficult time. All marriages, Christian or not, go through struggles. The first few years take such major adjustments.

What I had basically been ready to do was use God as an excuse not to deal with the problems. By using Him, I would somehow be able to justify breaking up my marriage. If I were "in pursuit of His will" then somehow it would be okay to "put asunder" what no man was supposed to "put asunder."

Before I alienate all of those who have been through the devastation of divorce, please allow me to interject that I believe every man and woman must seek God for himself or herself, concerning their relationship. There are some cases, in which there is abuse or adultery, where all choice has really been taken away from the injured party. I am not addressing this type of situation. What I am addressing is divorce for the sake of ease or want. "My life would be so much easier." "I could do what I wanted to do, if only…" "He is never going to be what I need." "He's just not what I want for my life." Funny, he was when you married him.

Where am I going with this? I just want you to know that marriages can have difficult times and still come out intact on the other side. God is a marvelous, creative God. He has ways of bringing healing and restoration that we could never even begin to fathom.

In those days, I could never have imagined the relationship that God would build between my husband and I. He fulfills me in every way. God knit us together in such a beautiful way that I cannot possibly imagine a life without him. Had I listened to the lies of the enemy on that day so long ago, I would have missed one of the greatest blessings of my life.

God changes everything.

Did you know that you can pray for God to increase your love for your spouse and He will do it? Did you know that He could increase your sex drive if you ask Him, so that you and your husband/wife are more compatible in this area?

Have you prayed about this lately?

He is a big God and He wants your marriage to succeed and be fulfilling *for your sake*. He was willing to make every sacrifice so that you would have access to healing and wholeness, fullness of life – whether for life in general, or in your marriage specifically. He is interested in what is going on behind the doors of your home.

Invite Him in. Make Him the center of your marriage, and watch things begin to change. It may not be overnight, but you have a Father who loves you enough to stay in it until the process is completed. I pray that you and your spouse can do the same. It is so worth it, my friend. Not only is it worth it, it is His will concerning you.

Questions or comments concerning today's lesson:

Day 3

Reality and Fantasy

Fantasy

The house is beautiful, just the way you'd always imagined it would be. The marble columns adorning the front porch and second story veranda glisten as the water from the reflecting pool catches the sun, splashing rosy color across their smooth surface. As you walk the length of the porch, toward the white wicker swing, your gauzy white dress whispers around your ankles, the breeze catches your waist-length curls causing them to dance around your perfectly sculpted face. The leaded crystal goblet in your hand feels cool against your lips, as you lift it and sip your julep (non-alcoholic, of course).

You look out across your perfectly manicured lawn – the magnolias lush and fragrant – and watch your children run to and fro, laughing as they delight in each other's company. Their pristine, expensive clothes look as if they had been hand tailored for each child. But wait; *that's right*, you laugh, *they were*!

As you lean back in the swing you hear the familiar hum of a small, exquisitely made motor coming from just beyond the very ornate, wrought iron security gate – it's his car, the Jaguar. *That car sounds nothing like my Mercedes*, you think to yourself. Soon, he is there, stepping out of the car he has left in the circular drive (you know the valet will take care of it).

When you see him, your heart begins to pound within your chest. You stand and start toward him. He smiles, beautiful white teeth a starling contrast to the deep tan that graces his face, and you are swept into his embrace. Your tuck your head into the warm curve of his neck and smell the clean, expensive cologne you gave him earlier that day. Your hearts beat in unison as you hold one another there upon the front porch of your perfect home. The children come bounding up the steps – one boy, one girl – to greet their much adored, much missed father. They place their small hands within yours. You turn, as the maid opens the front door, calling that your dinner will soon be served. Hand in hand, perfect smiles on perfect faces, you enter your perfect house where you will spend another perfect evening with your perfect family…just being perfect.

Reality

The house will never be in order again! You can't even imagine what it would look like clean. The dust webs in the corners of the awning glisten as the stagnate water in the plastic birdbath – lower half broken and lying beside the front step – reflects the light from yet another hubcap speeding past your curb. As you walk the length of the concrete patio, heading toward your metal fold-out chair, stumbling over big wheels, tricycles and dismembered Barbie-dolls, your gray sweat suit feels tight around your swollen ankles, the breeze catches your rollers, causing one to come loose and hang haphazardly beside the one eye you happened to have time to put mascara on that morning. The crack in the plastic Hardee's cup gets hung on your lip as you take that first sip of red Kool-Aid.

You look out into your brown lawn – the crabgrass lush and fragrant – and watch your children run to and fro, screaming frantically as they delight in tormenting one another. Their dusty, clearance rack clothes look as if they were made for someone else. But wait; *that's right*, you laugh, *they were! I put the other child's clothes on this one!*

As you lean back against the hot metal back of the chair, you hear the familiar clankety-clank of a rebuilt motor coming from just beyond the overgrown bush that blocks your view of the gravel driveway. It's his truck, the lemon. *That car sounds nothing like my Pinto*, you think to yourself. Soon, he is there, stepping out of the cloud of dust his truck left. When you see him your heart begins to pound (lack of oxygen from all the dust). You stand - your plump legs painfully peeling away from the metal chair – and start toward him. He smiles, beautiful white tooth a startling contrast to the dust filled creases that grace his face, and you stumble over the soccer ball, into his embrace. Your head lobs forward, banging painfully into his sweaty collarbone. You smell the familiar scent of the baby spit-up your daughter had given him earlier in the day. Your hearts beat in unison as you hold one another there on the patio, knowing that any moment now, the children will bound across the hay-like lawn, to harass their over-worked, very tired father. They gallop forward, placing their slug encrusted hands within your onion and green pepper smelling one. You turn as your brother-in-law opens the front door, calling out "There's something burning in here!" Hands reaching, frantic looks on well-worn faces, you enter your chaotic house, where you will spend another hour making another dinner, for a family that will probably not eat it anyway. Just perfect!

Okay, perhaps I exaggerated just a bit! The purpose of this exercise was not to be accurate and precise, but to get your attention. Why? Because I know beyond a shadow of a doubt that none of us will ever have a perfect life. I also believe that, for most of us, our lives are not nearly as bad as we make them out to be. We are such a blessed people. Unfortunately, we can also be a very greedy, covetous people. Some husband gives his wife a beautiful ring for their anniversary and all of a sudden, "Well, my husband never gets me anything like that!" While all along your husband has worked faithfully to provide for all of your needs. Your best friend purchases a new home and instead of joy, you are faced with a jealousy you had not expected. "I have more children than she does! She doesn't need that big house!" Your home is clean, warm, and meets your needs, but suddenly you are no longer thankful.

We catch glimpses of our hearts when those around us prosper and we feel that we are not.

Why am I saying all of this? Because the man who bought the beautiful ring for your friend just might be trying to make up for infidelity. The new house may be the only "affection" your friend is ever shown. You do not know what goes on behind the doors of anyone's home. When you covet what someone else has, you covet a lie, for no one knows what a person truly possesses, save the Lord.

Satan loves to make everyone else's marriage look better than yours. Strategically placed gifts, and overheard tender words can leave you "wishing my husband were like that." What a joke. What a lie! There is only one perfect husband, and that is Christ Himself, and this perfect Christ has ordained your marriage.

> *Be happy, yes, rejoice in the wife of your youth. Let her breasts and tender embrace satisfy you. Let her love alone fill you with delight. Why delight yourself with prostitutes, embracing what isn't yours? For God is closely watching you, and he weighs carefully everything you do.*
>
> Prov 5:18-21 (TLB)

My sisters, "Be happy, yes, rejoice in the husband you have loved since you were young. Let his strong embrace satisfy you. Let his love alone fill you with delight. Why find pleasure in and desire that which does not belong to you. God is watching you. He ponders all that you do."

I love all of you so much! Know that I am praying for your marriages, for they are precious in the sight of the Lord.

Questions or comments concerning today's lesson:

Day 4

The Word on Marriage

Okay, you knew this had to be coming. How in the world could you possibly talk about marriage for a whole week and not get to this point? Fasten your seatbelts, and reign in those feministic spirits, this is what the Word has to say about your marriage (I feel like Joe Friday on "Dragnet". "Just the facts Ma'am.").

> *Wives, submit to your husbands as to the Lord. For the husband is the head of the wife as Christ is the head of the church, his body, of which he is the Savior. Now as the church submits to Christ, so also wives should submit to their husbands in everything. Husbands, love your wives, just as Christ loved the church and gave himself up for her to make her holy, cleansing her by the washing with water through the word, and to present her to himself as a radiant church, without stain or wrinkle or any other blemish, but holy and blameless. In this same way, husbands ought to love their wives as their own bodies. He who loves his wife loves himself. After all, no one ever hated his own body, but he feeds and cares for it, just as Christ does the church-for we are members of his body.*
> *"For this reason a man will leave his father and mother and be united to his wife, and the two will become one flesh."*
> *This is a profound mystery-- but I am talking about Christ and the church. However, each one of you also must love his wife as he loves himself, and the wife must respect her husband.*
>
> Ephesians 5:22-33 (NIV)

Had enough? But wait…there's more!

> *Honor your marriage and its vows, and be pure; for God will surely punish all those who are immoral or commit adultery. Stay away from the love of money; be satisfied with what you have. For God has said, "I will never, never fail you nor forsake you."*
>
> Hebrews 13:4, 5 (TLB)

> *Their wives must be thoughtful, not heavy drinkers, not gossipers, but faithful in everything they do.*
>
> 1 Timothy 3:11 (TLB)

And now, for the Ginsu knives.

> *Wives, in the same way be submissive to your husbands so that, if any of them do not believe the word, they may be won over without words by the behavior of their wives, when they see*

> *the purity and reverence of your lives. Your beauty should not come from outward adornment, such as braided hair and the wearing of gold jewelry and fine clothes.*
>
> *Instead, it should be that of your inner self, the unfading beauty of a gentle and quiet spirit, which is of great worth in God's sight. For this is the way the holy women of the past who put their hope in God used to make themselves beautiful. They were submissive to their own husbands, like Sarah, who obeyed Abraham and called him her master. You are her daughters if you do what is right and do not give way to fear.*
>
> *Husbands, in the same way be considerate as you live with your wives, and treat them with respect as the weaker partner and as heirs with you of the gracious gift of life, so that nothing will hinder your prayers.*
>
> *Finally, all of you, live in harmony with one another; be sympathetic, love as brothers, be compassionate and humble. Do not repay evil with evil or insult with insult, but with blessing, because to this you were called so that you may inherit a blessing. For, "Whoever would love life and see good days must keep his tongue from evil and his lips from deceitful speech. He must turn from evil and do good; he must seek peace and pursue it. For the eyes of the Lord are on the righteous and his ears are attentive to their prayer, but the face of the Lord is against those who do evil."*
>
> *Who is going to harm you if you are eager to do good? But even if you should suffer for what is right, you are blessed. "Do not fear what they fear; do not be frightened." But in your hearts set apart Christ as Lord. Always be prepared to give an answer to everyone who asks you to give the reason for the hope that you have. But do this with gentleness and respect, keeping a clear conscience, so that those who speak maliciously against your good behavior in Christ may be ashamed of their slander.*
>
> 1 Peter 3:1-16 (NIV)

So, what now?

> *Let us, therefore, make every effort to enter that rest, so that no one will fall by following their example of disobedience. For the word of God is living and active. Sharper than any double-edged sword, it penetrates even to dividing soul and spirit, joints and marrow; it judges the thoughts and attitudes of the heart.*
>
> Hebrews 4:11, 12 (NIV)

Allow the Word of God to penetrate your heart this day. Go back and read the Scripture passages and make note of any behavior your may be holding onto that does not line up with the Word concerning your part of your marriage. The tendency, at this point, would be to say, a few "But he's…" But let's not do that. *You* allow the Holy Spirit to speak to *your* heart, and line yourself up with the Word. God is well able to speak to any heart out there that needs to be next.

On that note, we will Selah (pause calmly and think upon these things). Feel free to go over today's lesson anytime you need an "attitude adjustment."

Questions or comments concerning today's lesson:

Day 5

Putting It All Together

Today we are going to enjoy our final teaching on marriage. I have enjoyed laughing with you and saying a few "Ouch, Hallelujah's!" as we have explored basic truth's concerning marriage. I cannot in good conscience, however, close this chapter out without addressing one more area of marriage.

Your first clue…

> "One night as I was sleeping, my heart awakened in a dream. I heard the voice of my beloved; he was knocking at my bedroom door. 'Open to me, my darling, my lover, my lovely dove,' he said, 'for I have been out in the night and am covered with dew.'
> "But I said, 'I have disrobed. Shall I get dressed again? I have washed my feet, and should I get them soiled?'
> "My beloved tried to unlatch the door, and my heart was thrilled within me. I jumped up to open it, and my hands dripped with perfume, my fingers with lovely myrrh as I pulled back the bolt."
>
> Song of Solomon 5:2-5 (TLB)

You do not need another clue, do you? Didn't think so!

It is time to unlock the door, girlfriend. Time to dab a little Chanel #5 behind the ears, and look for that silky little bit of cloth you used to call a "nightie." Your beloved has knocked long enough; it is time to let your heart be "thrilled at the thought of him."

"Why, I can't believe you're going to talk about this in a Bible study." Believe it!

Here we go…

Which of the following attitudes best describes you?

- "Sex is just something else I have to do before I get to sleep at the end of the day."
- "God says I have to, so I guess I have to."
- "This is an opportunity to show my husband how much I love him." (I heard that! You said, "Yeah, right!")

All of you who answered yes to the latter, you may now shut your book. As for the rest of you, stay with me just a little while longer. God wants more for you. Notice I did not say *from* you.

The man should give his wife all that is her right as a married woman, and the wife should do the same for her husband:

> *For a girl who marries no longer has full right to her own body, for her husband then has his rights to it, too; and in the same way the husband no longer has full right to his own body, for it belongs also to his wife. So do not refuse these rights to each other. The only exception to this rule would be the agreement of both husband and wife to refrain from the rights of marriage for a limited time, so that they can give themselves more completely to prayer. Afterwards, they should come together again so that Satan won't be able to tempt them because of their lack of self-control.*
>
> 1 Corinthians 7:3-5 (TLB)

God addresses the area of physical need in quite an emphatic way. He makes it very clear that we are not to deprive one another of this "right." I know there are women reading right now that cringe at the thought of someone having a "right" to their body. I understand. Really I do. I know that many of you have faced abusive situations that cause you to want to protect yourself from all things physical, but know this; you do not have to fear what God has ordained as good. Your body was intended to give and receive pleasure within the covenant of marriage. Your physical makeup gives evidence to God's intent concerning this aspect of your marriage. You are perfectly fit to your husband, and he to you. It is okay to enjoy, yes, I said enjoy, your sexuality with your husband.

Sex and Christianity are not mutually exclusive. You do not have to give up one to fully participate in the other.

You are fearfully and wonderfully made, and part of the wonder of your creation is the intricately woven pattern of need, desire, pleasure and faithfulness with which you were knit together. God made no mistake when He created woman with the capacity to respond to the touch of her husband's hand. It was no fluke of nature that caused a man to be able to look at his wife and long to be intimate with her. He created us with a wonderfully compelling desire for physical intimacy with our mate. It is okay! It really is a good thing.

The world has taken the beautiful Truth concerning sexual intimacy within marriage and distorted it, as it does all Truth. What was intended to be holy has been made unclean. What God intended for good, they have used for evil. We have been bombarded with sexual imagery that causes us, as Christians, to unfortunately see sex as something for the carnal. Just remember, no matter what the world does, God's intent does not change. He has not changed His mind about the gift He has given, just because someone else has chosen to misuse it.

You not only have His permission, you have His encouragement, to enjoy a healthy sexual relationship with your husband or wife.

Okay, just one more thing.

For all of you who are trying to jump on the part of the verse that says you can separate yourself for a time of prayer - that month long prayer vigil you are planning, as we speak, is not going to cut it! Neither do I believe that "pray without ceasing" would be appropriate here.

In all seriousness, do not withhold yourself from one another. Frequent, passionate lovemaking is essential, (yes, *essential* – not optional) in creating a healthy marriage. Great protection from the temptations of the evil one can be found in the open, welcoming arms of our beloved. So, as King Solomon advises,

> *"Oh, lover and beloved eat and drink! Yes, drink deeply!"*
>
> Song of Solomon 5:1 (TLB)

I know I said one more thing, but there is an addendum I simply must make. There is much to be said for creativity and spontaneity in this area of your marriage. If you are bored, there is a reason. The principle we spoke of last week would apply here: Want to get more out of your relationship, you have to give more. Need a few ideas? Read Song of Solomon.

And here we will once again. Selah!

Questions or comments concerning today's lesson:

Commissioned

"My hope is fading swift, My Lord,
How can I the standard meet?"
"Tis not so far to climb, dear child,
When sitting at My feet."

Lofty thoughts soon come to heel,
Troubled minds find rest,
While lying close to hear His heart resound,
"Just do your best."

"But Lord, my best has never been,
Acceptable thus far."
"You've sought the wrong opinions, child.
You are grand just as you are."

"More than I have created,
Child, do not strive to be.
The gifts you have flow easily,
They are a gift from Me.

If what you do seems difficult,
Beyond this peace of mind,
Search your heart for motives true,
Your answers you will find.
For what I've placed within you,

Flows directly from My throne,
The ease with which you translate,
Tells if source be Me alone.
So, dear child, let rivers run,

Let My Spirit be swift spread,
Upon the wounded, crying soul,
That you touch in My stead.
Be tendered by emotions,

That at times do overwhelm.
Listen to your Spirits heart,
Discern this soulish realm.
Call white as white and black as black,

No grays your sight will see.
For quite distinctive is the difference,
Between this world and Me.
A counterfeit to meet each circumstance,

You're sure to face.
Look to Me to wisdom grant,
Depend upon My grace.
Speak what you hear and see of Me,

No words from others speak.
Be careful of the sinful pride,
Make sure it's Me you seek.
For much I give into your hands,

My call, a price will pay,
But with it comes greatest reward,
'Twill all be yours someday.
For now, though, heart be quite content,

To seek My face and grow.
Patience learn, peace do plant,
Mind all seeds you sow.
Expect the least expected,

For you know not this place.
You've cried for it, fought hard for it,
But never seen a trace.
Surprise, My child, Surprise, I bring,

Your heart wants more, it's true,
But you cannot even fathom,
The plans I have for you!
My thoughts are so much higher,

Than what you could yet perceive,
I ask but small concession,
Daughter you must believe.
Believe Me when the circumstance,

Says this cannot be true.
Believe Me child, then stand back,
And see what your God can do."
You have been commissioned...

CLASS NOTES

Week Six

I Wish Someone Had Told Me About Satan's Mind Games

"For who among men knows the thoughts of a man except the man's spirit within him?"
1 Corinthians 2:11(NIV)

Day 1
Footholds

Day 2
Strongholds

Day 3
Confusion and a Double-Mind

Day 4
Torments and Evil Forebodings

Day 5
A Sound Mind

Of all the subjects we will address in this ten-week study, this hits the closest to home. Struggling with your thought-life can be such a devastating experience. This is where Satan wages his battles. This is his turf of choice, for this is where we, as Christians, tend to let down our guard. "It's just a thought, right?" "It's not like I would ever *do* anything." We fool ourselves into believing the things we watch, read, listen to and think about, make no difference. "After all," we rationalize; "it is not as if I am hurting anyone." My friends, when we begin to actually believe that, we are well on our way to bondages that only divine intervention can break. The Apostle James states it plainly:

> *"But each one is tempted when, by his own evil desire, he is dragged away and enticed. Then, after desire has conceived, it gives birth to sin; and sin, when it is full-grown, gives birth to death. Don't be deceived, my dear brothers."*
>
> James 1:14-16

This week we will expose some of the schemes of the enemy.

> *"Behold, I send you out as sheep in the midst of wolves; therefore be shrewd as serpents, and innocent as doves."*
>
> Matthew 10:16 (NAS)

Day 1

Footholds

Be ye angry, and sin not: let not the sun go down upon your wrath: Neither give place to the devil.

Ephesians 4:26-27 (KJV)

"If you are angry, don't sin by nursing your grudge. Don't let the sun go down with you still angry-- get over it quickly; for when you are angry, you give a mighty foothold to the devil."

Ephesians 4:26-27 (TLB)

Read I Peter 5:6-11 and answer the following questions.

What is the first thing we are told to do in verse 6?

_____
_____
_____
_____

Why are we to humble ourselves?

_____
_____
_____
_____

What are we told to do in verse 7?

_____
_____
_____
_____

Why?

_____
_____
_____
_____

Verse 8 tells us to be _____ and _____. Because our enemy_____ _____ prowls around looking for someone to _____. Because of this, verse 9 gives us a warning to _____ _____ and _____ _____ _____ in the faith.

We are to resist him, or as it says in Ephesians 4:26, "*give him no place.*"

The word "place," translated as *foothold* in Ephesians 4:26, is topos (top'-os) in the Greek/Hebrew. It is defined as "a spot (general in space, but limited by occupancy)."

Look for just a moment at the definition you just read, specifically the "limited by occupancy" part. You know what that says to me? It tells me that if you run him off, the "place" no longer belongs to him. It has not yet become a stronghold. It is merely a place where he is trying to dig in his heels. This probably sounds really strange, but this definition makes me smile. It gives me hope. So many of us have been lied to by the enemy, told we would never be free of the bondages we have allowed him to create in our lives. But I believe some of you are going to be set free by the thought that he only has a foothold; and that is contingent upon him occupying the space. I hope that makes you want to stand up and give a mighty shove in the spirit realm. I hope that helps you recognize one of his schemes. You know the one; it says, "I am in control and you have no power over this area of your life any longer." Oh, dear one, next time you hear that voice, see it coming from an old goat trying to hang onto the side of a mountain. He is yelling at the top of his lungs trying to scare you into immobility, when all he has is his front hooves dug into the earth for balance. One shove, given from the depths of your spirit, based on the Truth of Scripture, can send him tumbling and spinning right back to where he came from.

A foothold is always the beginning of the scenario. It is not Satan's ultimate goal; it is merely his means to an end. That is why it is so important that you do as you were told in 1 Peter 5:8 and resist him. Do not listen to his lies. He will convince you that you are in bondage before he ever gets the first rope around you.

I am reminded of some friends who had a dog who absolutely relished his freedom. Every time they opened the door this dog would take off, full-tilt-boogie. I mean this was one active, happy, uncontainable critter. While my friends enjoyed the vivacious spirit of the dog, they did not enjoy chasing him around the countryside, so they bought an invisible fence.

They installed the monitors on the perimeter or their property and put a special collar on the dog that would give him a tiny jolt when he attempted to cross those boundaries. After a very short time, the dog no longer even tried to leave the yard. He had experienced the unpleasant results of trying to break free and gave up his pursuit of freedom. The family was then able to turn the fence off, disconnect it completely, and the dog would not leave the yard. Why? Because he was convinced of his captivity, and did not want to pay the price to get free. He was held in check by something that no longer existed.

Do you see where I am headed with this? Satan has convinced us that there is something keeping us in this place of bondage. He has convinced us of this by thwarting our efforts repeatedly with lies and more lies. Each time we attempted to break free, his lies sent a jolt of fear through our hearts and we eventually gave up. We have become disappointed, angry and full of shame because we have not broken free. We are held in captivity because a liar told us the fence was on.

The irony of the situation is quite striking. If that dog had decided it wanted to leave, even when the fence was on, it would have experienced a fraction of a second of discomfort, then it would have been able to go anywhere it wanted to go. It amazes me that even the smallest amount of suffering in the flesh can cause us to stay in bondage for the rest of our lives. If God is telling you to do something to get free, whatever it may be, do it.

Write 2 Corinthians 4:17 in the space provided.

_____
_____
_____
_____

Please do not allow eternal things to be set aside by temporary suffering in the flesh. You can be free of habitual sin if you will simply decide to say no to the lusts of the flesh. Do not give Satan a place. Remember it is only his when you allow him to occupy it. Kick him out! Take back what the enemy has stolen. My precious friend, *there is no fence!*

Has the Lord shown you that there are places where you have given Satan a foothold? If so, list them below.

_____
_____
_____
_____

If you have areas that need to be reclaimed, it is time for you to take them back. There is an anointing (the anointing breaks the yoke) for freedom available to you at this very moment. God has brought you here for a reason, and that reason is freedom!

> *"It is for freedom that Christ has set us free. Stand firm, then, and do not let yourselves be burdened again by a yoke of slavery."*
>
> Galations 5:1 (NIV)

Go through your list and speak to the enemy concerning the *place* he is trying to occupy. Tell him to leave in the name of Jesus. Do what we are commanded to do in 1 Peter 5:9, resist him! (Resist: to fight against; withstand; oppose: as in to resist an invasion) Do not let him maintain his foothold, for footholds become strongholds. Give him *no place to stand*.

Questions or comments concerning today's lesson:

Day 2

Strongholds

The LORD is my light and my salvation-- whom shall I fear? The LORD is the stronghold of my life - of whom shall I be afraid?

Psalm 27:1

From the very beginning of time, God was supposed to be the only stronghold of your life. What is a stronghold? Webster's defines a stronghold as "a well fortified place." What did we say about the word *place* yesterday? Remember we talked about occupancy. If you need to refresh your memory, briefly review yesterday's lesson. "Well fortified" – built up, made strong, strengthened against attack.

This is either a really good thing or a really bad thing for you, depending upon what manner of stronghold you have in your life at this moment. If Christ is your one and only stronghold, you are strengthened against attack. If Satan has maintained his foothold long enough to climb onto firm ground and take up residence, have no doubt, he is building a fortress of lies with which he will be strengthened against attack. Every time you believe the lies, his fortress becomes stronger. He will not give up ground or back down no matter what you do in the flesh. So, do we just give up since the enemy will give up no ground? Absolutely not!

He shall say, "Hear, O Israel, today you are going into battle against your enemies. Do not be fainthearted or afraid; do not be terrified or give way to panic before them. For the LORD your God is the one who goes with you to fight for you against your enemies to give you victory."

Deuteronomy 20:3, 4

Read 1 Samuel 17:47.

This battle is not going to be won by anything you do. It will be won by total dependence upon the Only One Who is able to bring complete victory to your battle. God will do it and He alone will get the glory. He will give your enemy into your hands! Once you have your hands on him, here is what the Word says to do.

Write 2 Corinthians 10:3-5 in the space provided.

_____
_____
_____
_____

We do not wage war as the world does. The weapons we fight with have been given divine power to demolish strongholds. The word *weapon* used in this passage is keliy (kel-ee'). It means, "something *prepared* to fight with."

We do not fight as the world fights. Our greatest weapon is the Word. We fight with the Sword of the Word. We have the Word hidden in our hearts and available to confront the lies of the enemy. The Word PREPARES us for battle. We have weapons, but we must have them at the ready.

Ephesians 6:10-18 is a familiar passage of scripture, but I want you to read every word. Do not be tempted to skip over what is familiar. If you are engaged in overthrowing strongholds, you must do it through and by the Holy Spirit of God. Let him prepare you with the Word of truth.

> *"Last of all I want to remind you that your strength must come from the Lord's mighty power within you. Put on all of God's armor so that you will be able to stand safe against all strategies and tricks of Satan. For we are not fighting against people made of flesh and blood, but against persons without bodies, the evil rulers of the unseen world, those mighty satanic beings and great evil princes of darkness who rule this world; and against huge numbers of wicked spirits in the spirit world. So use every piece of God's armor to resist the enemy whenever he attacks, and when it is all over, you will still be standing up. However, to do this, you will need the strong belt of truth and the breastplate of God's approval. Wear shoes that are able to speed you on as you preach the Good News of peace with God. In every battle, you will need faith as your shield to stop the fiery arrows aimed at you by Satan. Moreover, you will need the helmet of salvation and the sword of the Spirit, which is the Word of God. Pray all the time. Ask God for anything in line with the Holy Spirit's wishes. Plead with him, reminding him of your needs, and keep praying earnestly for all Christians everywhere."*

Ephesians 6:10-18 (TLB)

I believe Paul admonished us to pray for Christians everywhere because he knew we would all be faced with the exact same trials and tribulations. Satan has no new tricks. He does not need them because we have yet to overcome the old ones. He does the same thing over and over and it works for him. That is why we have fathers and sons addicted to drugs, mothers and daughters fighting depression, whole families fighting gluttony and obesity. Same old scheme, different person.

We must tear down the strongholds of the enemy in our lives or our children will be fighting our battles after we have gone.

Christ died on the cross to give you access to the very Throne of God. Call out to Him! Make your petition known to your God. Throw yourself at His feet and ask Him to forgive you for the rebellion that led you into captivity in the first place. Repent and turn away from habitual sin. Renew your mind with the Word of God and walk in the Truth you have gained.

David gave in to lust and was almost destroyed by the ramifications of his rebellious sin. However, we see him return to the Lord with a repentant heart, and he is able to say with all conviction, "The LORD is the stronghold of my life - of whom shall I be afraid?"

About Satan's Mind Games

Satan is a liar. Even now, he is attacking your mind with reminders of your captivity. He is telling you how many times you failed to bring down this stronghold in the past. Do not listen! He is afraid of the Truth that you have gained through the Word. He knows his defeat will come through the Word alone. Now that you have him down, do as David did after bringing Goliath down; take off the head of your enemy. Do not let him rise to do battle again.

Be free, in the name of Jesus!

May He and He alone, be the stronghold of your life.

Questions or comments concerning today's lesson:

Too Much

"Here we go again," persistent cry of double-mind
"Oh, I know, I know the answer," but somehow, it is hard to find.
"I've decided now, but then again, maybe I'm not sure."
I set my sight only to find I am drawn by subtle lure.

"You didn't really hear His voice, it could've been your own."
Whispered torments, questions raised, confusions wind is blown.
"Make up your mind! Are you so weak, your thoughts you cannot control?"
Constant reminders, taunting cries, such torment to my soul.

Why can't my heart for all time set on what I know is true?
Why can't I lift petitions, knowing the answer comes from You?
What have I let my mind come to? What seeds have deep been sown?
Childish places trod by one who should be quite full-grown.

Can I get it back, dear Lord? Can I make the torment cease?
"When you give it all to Me, you will find your peace.
You were not called as others, your call is quite unique.
You cannot serve as others serve. Child, daily your must seek,

My face, My hand, My favor, My peace, My yoke, My will,
Nothing else will ever encompass the void you try to fill.
Confusion claims its victims when they are least aware,
Minds occupied with foolishness, and eyes not set with care.

You do not guard that which I give, you cast aside with ease.
You look for smiling, easy words and lies so sure to please.
You disregard the truth you know, desires do rule your walk,
You have turned your mouth to idle things, no faith left in your talk.

If it is the truth you are seeking here, not mere scratch of itching ears,
Listen close, I'll give to you the wisdom of My years.
Oh, but wait, I've done just that. My Word has come to you,
It's all laid out, your answers there, you know what you must do.

Set time aside, make Me the first thing that you crave each day,
My words will fill you, My love soon heal you, and send you on your way.
Your life is so much more than days long spent on eat and drink.
Your victory lies in everything you do and say and think.

So set your mind on higher things, seek Me always first,
Single minded you'll become, then I can quench your thirst.
You're not hungry for the food you eat, you're hungry for my touch,
But when I reach, you run from Me, crying, "Oh it's just too much!"

Too much is what you're wearing on the heart I gave to you.
Too much is watching a child of mine be beaten black and blue.
Too much is seeing My own Son be nailed high on a tree,
So you can turn, live life your way, come running back to Me!

The mess is made, now clean it up! The tools are in your hand.
Dry tears from face! I've given grace! Now you must make a stand!"

Questions or comments concerning today's lesson:

Day 3

Confusion and a Double Mind

"For God is not the author of confusion but of peace."

1 Corinthians 14:33 NKJ

Read James 1 and complete the following.

What must finish its work so you may be mature and complete, lacking nothing?
_____

Verse 5 tells us if we are lacking in wisdom we should ask God, and that He will give generously without finding fault. Why do you think it was important for God to make it clear that He would not "find fault" with us when we asked?
_____
_____
_____

"But when he asks he must _____ and not _____, because he who _____ is like a wave of the sea, blown and _____ by the wind. That man should not think he will _____ _____ from the Lord; he is a _____ - _____ man, _____ in all he does."

What does verse 12 tell us about the man who perseveres?
_____
_____
_____

Please write verses 14-16 in the space provided
_____
_____
_____

Verse 16 should stand out like a neon sign. There is so much behind those words. *"Don't be deceived my dear brothers."* One small sentence that, when applied to our lives, revolutionizes our walk with God. We have to stop listening to the lies of the enemy! Deception is his forté. It always has been and always will be. However, Satan is not the only one prone to deception around here. Take a look at verse 22.

Interesting, huh?

Many of the things we give Satan credit for have very little to do with him, and much to do with our own evil desires. Look back at verses 14-16. Do you see what is taking place in this scenario? We have sin issues in our lives that we want to lay at the feet of the enemy, when the issue should be laid at our own feet. We give our minds free reign to take us places where we never should go. We play with thoughts and ideas that should have been rejected the moment they popped into our little brains. We go around rebuking and rebuking when what we really need to do is just quit walking in the sin for which we keep rebuking Satan.

Somewhere along the way, we have given ourselves a scapegoat in the form of a devil. We have become less responsible for our behavior if, as Flip Wilson used to say, "The devil made me do it." But you know what, the seventy-two returned with joy and said,

> *"Lord, even the demons submit to us in your name." He replied, "I saw Satan fall like lightning from heaven. I have given you authority to trample on snakes and scorpions and to overcome all the power of the enemy; nothing will harm you."*
>
> Luke 10:17-19

God has given us authority over our enemies - all of them! That "demon" causing you to walk in sins of the flesh, may very well just be a lack of disciplining your own flesh and bringing it into submission to the authority of God. You do not have to be demon-possessed to sin. Nor do you have to be "oppressed" (religious catchword of the day) by the enemy.

Our own choices often lead us into or out of captivity.

Satan is a liar, and he is a bully. He assumes power that he does not have, and unless you know that the power is yours alone to give him, he will walk all over you every time. The only power he will ever have over you will be the power you give him. It is very much the same as Pilate and Jesus, when Pilate asked him to speak and Jesus refused. Pilate became angry and said, (I am paraphrasing) "Don't you know I have the power to kill you or set you free?" Jesus answered him and said, "The only power you have, you have because my Father has given it to you."

Okay, here is the actual scripture.

> *"Do you refuse to speak to me?" Pilate said. "Don't you realize I have power either to free you or to crucify you?" Jesus answered, "You would have no power over me if it were not given to you from above."*
>
> John 19:10, 11

We have already established in Luke 10 that we have been given authority over anything – did you hear me – *anything* the enemy brings our way. There is nothing greater than the authority placed within you by God. Sounds kind of like "Greater is He that is in you than he that is in the world," huh?

Let's bring this thing together.

God establishes in James that His people should be a stedfast kind of people. We have been called to persevere, to be established and unmovable in all things. We have been created with the capacity to grasp the Truth then hold on for dear life, literally. Satan's scheme is to get us to begin to rethink the truth that we have inside of us. He plants seeds of doubt, seeds of disappointment, seeds of frustration and we begin to search for answers different from the ones we know to be truth. We look for easier ways to get there and arrive at our final destination. Satan gets us focused on formulas and plans and we begin to get confused.

Confusion is birthed when you attempt to compromise the truth of the Word with the truth of the world. You try to convince yourself that God meant something other than what is actually written in the Word.

Double-mindedness takes root when you know the Truth, but refuse to walk it out in your flesh. This is rebellion, which is as the sin of witchcraft. Your flesh begins to live by one set of standards, while your spirit longs to walk in the Truth. You have now given birth to a double-mind that will keep you unstable in everything you do!

Okay, so why did I start with the first chapter of James? Because bringing our minds into submission to God's authority is going to take perseverance. The word used in James 1:4, translated as perseverance is: hupomone (hoop-om-on-ay'); cheerful (or hopeful) endurance, constancy: enduring, patience, patient continuance (waiting).

This "changing of the guard" over your mind will have to be walked out. Unless God performs a radical miracle – which He is well able to do, should He so choose – you will be walking this one out until He comes for us. Your first order of business? Know the Truth.

Once you know the Truth, do not let anyone or anything sway you from that Truth. Take back your mind! Do not let Satan torment you one moment longer with, "Yeah, but…"

> *"You will know the Truth and the Truth will set you free."*
>
> John 8:32

Free your mind to the Word of God. Set it free to take in as much scriptural wisdom as you can. There is life and peace in the Word.

> *For this reason I remind you to fan into flame the gift of God, which is in you through the laying on of my hands. For God did not give us a spirit of timidity, but a spirit of power, of love and of self-discipline.*
>
> 2 Timothy 1:6, 7

Sophronismos (so-fron-is-mos'); discipline, i.e. self-control: KJV - sound mind.

A Personal Note: Satan has been trying to convince many of you that you are on the verge of losing everything; your mind, your family, your salvation, but do not believe him. Remember, he is a liar. God has given you a sound mind and you can do everything you need to do to live a full productive life. Speak the Word out loud to your accuser. Tell him that God has given you a sound mind and has made provision for you. Believe the Word, my friend. You are not "losing it." Satan has already lost it all.

Questions or comments concerning today's lesson:

Day 4

Dread, Worry and Torment

"There they were, overwhelmed with dread, where there was nothing to dread."

Psalm 53:5

I sat in my dentist's chair waiting nervously for the pain I knew was to come. There would be a couple of shots, a pinching of the abused area, as well as the scraping and drilling. I hated everything about the dentist (not him personally, but the uncomfortable experience he represented) and wanted to be anywhere but there. As my fingertips drummed nervously over the leather arm of the chair, my eyes trying to look anywhere save the shiny silver tray just entering my peripheral vision, I caught sight of a little picture upon the wall. Inside the frame was a caption that read *"Things I have learned…"* It was an excerpt from the writings of a 99-year-old woman. The first thing on the list was *"Ninety-nine percent of the things I worried about in my lifetime never came to pass."* I paused and thought about that for a moment. I was sure that anyone who had lived that long must have had many worries. I was also quite sure that she had to have wisdom that I did not posses after all of that time. So I thought a moment longer. She had come to realize how much time in her short life had been wasted on useless worries. She had walked out a Biblical Truth - you know the one that states,

"Who of you by worrying can add a single hour to his life? Since you cannot do this very little thing, why do you worry about the rest?"

Luke 12:25, 26

Dread and worry can absolutely drain you of every ounce of energy you have, both spiritual and physical. Solomon said it well:

"An anxious heart weighs a man down."

Proverbs 12:25

Dread, worry and anxiety are mindsets that we, as Christians, were never intended to have. Scripture is very emphatic about the casting off of such mental attacks. Let's look at three of these verses (there are too many to list them all). After you look up each reference, write the instruction given within the text. (i.e. "Do not be anxious…")

Philippians 4:6 _____

Matthew 6:25-34 _____

Luke 12:22 _____

There are also many scriptures that make it very clear that anxiety and fear were seen as an attack or curse. Worry and dread were never considered just part of life. Read the following and see what I mean.

Deuteronomy 28:65.

Exodus 15:16.

These verses tell us that we have allowed the enemy into an area of our lives that he was never intended to have. When we allow him to run rampant in our thought life, consuming every waking moment with worry, anxiety and dread, we lose our strength. We lose our focus on Christ and begin to walk in fear. We have no peace, our joy seems non-existent, and heaviness settles over us. Is that the way a son or daughter of God Almighty should live? Of course not! But we do it all of the time. By worrying and walking in fear we are disobeying a direct command of the Father. Isaiah said it quite eloquently. He told us that we are supposed to do things differently than the rest of the world.

> *"...do not fear what they fear, and do not dread it."*
>
> Isaiah 8:12

If fear is given into (which is exactly what worry is) for an extended period of time, torments and evil-forebodings (feelings that something bad is going to happen) begin to control the mind. The mind begins to run with the worst possible scenario (a headache is thought to be a brain tumor; a mole must be cancer). Our emotions run away with us because we have ceased to operate from a position of faith. We then become another victim of Satan's schemes.

When you have reached the stage of *torment* I would strongly suggest you seek counsel from your pastor, Christian counselor or someone you trust in spiritual matters. While you are capable of defeating the enemy on your own, mental strongholds can incapacitate your faith to such a degree that you need someone to stand with you and speak the Word of Truth into that area of attack. If you feel unable to seek counsel at this time, for whatever reason, enter into some serious Word time. Set aside a length of time (whatever the Lord may lay on your heart), and fast and pray. Seek Him. He knows what you are going through and will be there for you. Surround yourself with Truth and Light. Do not allow yourself to think about any situation in any way other than "what does the Word say about this." Consider only what the Word has to say about your situation. Begin to set mental boundaries for yourself. You alone know when your greatest moments of anxiety usually hit. Make sure you are armed with your Sword of the Spirit so that you may battle for your mind.

When I was a little girl (probably six years old), my home burned down. We lost everything. I remember standing in the front yard looking toward my bedroom, watching the flames consume the shelf that held all of my stuffed toys. I remember thinking they had all died. You know how the mind of a child works. After the fire I began to have nightmares. I suffered from nightmares so often that they became the norm for me. I hated going to sleep at night because I knew what awaited me when I closed my eyes. I could not tell anybody because I did not want to be a "baby," so I suffered in silence for the longest time. I prayed every night "Please God, don't let my house burn down. Please God, do not let my house burn down." I would place my favorite toys near the window, just in case I had to save them. I would cry myself to sleep. I was tormented by thoughts of impending evil. I just had a feeling something bad was going to happen. That feeling stayed with me for the longest time.

One night, after a particularly horrible dream, I woke up crying out for my mama. She came in and soothed me until I stopped crying and was calm enough to tell her about my dream. I told her how I had been having these nightmares "forever." She got up, went to her room, and came back in with her Bible.

She sat down and said, *"Barbie, you know that Jesus loves you?"*
"Yes," I sniffed.
"You know that I love you?"
"Uh huh," I rubbed at my eyes and wiped my nose on my sleeve.
"You know that takes care of those that He loves?"
"Uh huh."
"Okay then, we're gonna put this Bible under your pillow, 'cause it will remind you how much me and Jesus love you. When you feel this Bible you will know that nothing bad can come through that kind of love."

She tucked the Bible under the pillow (it raised my head quite a bit, since it was a "grown up Bible") and I felt safe for the first time in ages. She kissed me and padded off, her cotton gown looking more like superwoman's cape than anything I had ever seen. I slept like the babe that I was. Tormenting dreams left me from that night forward.

Was there magic in that old leather bound King James? No. There was faith in a love that my Savior had for me, and in the fact that my mama did not lie. Faith and love had joined hands and delivered me from torment's clutches.

I am thirty-six years old, and to this day, if I have a bad dream, I will reach over on my nightstand – still half-asleep- grab my Bible, tuck it under my pillow and drift off into the "sweet sleep" that I was promised in Proverbs:

"When you lie down, you will not be afraid; when you lie down, your sleep will be sweet."
Proverbs 3:24

Many of you are struggling with tormenting thoughts and I would just say to you, mix His love with your mustard seed faith and take back what the enemy has stolen.

"You will keep in perfect peace him whose mind is steadfast, because he trusts in you."
Isaiah 26:3

Questions or comments concerning today's lesson:

Day 5

A Sound Mind

"Thanks be to God – through Jesus Christ our Lord! So then, I myself in my mind am a slave to God's law."

Roman 7:25

"The mind of sinful man is death, but the mind controlled by the Spirit is life and peace; the sinful mind is hostile to God. It does not submit to God's law, nor can it do so."

Romans 8: 6, 7

"Do not conform any longer to the pattern of this world, but be transformed by the renewing of your mind. Then you will be able to test and approve what God's will is – his good, pleasing and perfect will."

Romans 12:2

"So what shall I do? I will pray with my spirit, but I will also pray with my mind; I will sing with my spirit, but I will also sing with my mind."

1 Corinthians 14:15

Fill in the blanks of Philippians 3:14-21.

"I press on toward _____ _____ to win the prize for which God has _____ _____ heavenward in Christ Jesus.

All of us who are _____ should take such a view of things. And if on some point you think differently, that too God will make _____ to you.

Only let us live up to what we have _____ _____.

Join with others in _____ _____ _____, brothers, and take note of those who live according to the _____ we gave you.

For, as I have often told you before and now say again even with tears, many live as _____ of the cross of Christ.

Their destiny is _____, their god is their _____, and their _____ is in their _____. Their _____ is on earthly things.

Their mind is on earthly things. Because they have their mind on earthly things they have begun to worship other gods (their stomach, koilia (koy-lee'-ah); figuratively, the heart: which tells us that they were being led by their feelings and emotions, rather than by the truth of the Word) and their destiny had become shame and destruction. Pretty harsh repercussions for thinking about worldly things! But if you look a little closer, you will see what Paul was actually saying.

Phroneo (fron-eh'-o); entertain (the mind) or have a sentiment, to be (mentally) disposed (more or less earnestly in a certain direction); intensively, to interest oneself in (with concern or obedience).

The Philippi people had not only begun to think about earthly things (concerns dealing with the flesh and the things with which to gratify please or sustain the flesh), they had become "entertained" by it. They were "intensely interested" in the things of the flesh realm. Their minds had been taken into "obedience" to the thought patterns of the world. That, is quite different than "Oh, it was just on my mind."

You will fall in love with what you think about all the time. What or whom do you think about first thing in the morning? What about last thing before you fall asleep at night? Do you know that your answer probably sheds a great deal of light on where your "treasure is?"

Read Matthew 6:21.

We think about the things that are important to us. That which consumes us occupies our minds. That which consumes our mind will soon control our spirit.

We must be so careful about keeping our thought life where it should be. God gave us a wonderful capacity for knowledge and discovery. He created us to be inquisitive and intrigued by what we do not know. These attributes were placed within us to bring about an earnest search for our Creator. We have been seekers of Truth from the very beginning. However, this search can lead us down paths best left untrod if we do not keep our mind unto Christ.

You must protect your mind with all diligence. Guard it as you would your heart. What you feed into your mind will determine how and what you think. And what you think, will determine who you are.

> *"The good man brings good things out of the good stored up in his heart, and the evil man brings evil things out of the evil stored up in his heart…"*
>
> Luke 6:45

> *"We have the mind of Christ."*
>
> I Corinthians 2:16b

We have been given the mind of Christ. The Mind of Christ! Did I mention that we have been given the *Mind of Christ!?* So what is our deal? Why do we allow the enemy to do the things he does with this Mind of Christ? God gave us a sound mind. He gave us a great capacity to learn and grow. He gave us everything we would need to live the life of an overcomer here in this sinful world. There is no weapon in Satan's arsenal that can take our sound mind unless we hand it to him. There is no lie big enough to overtake the Truth unless we choose to supplant it. There is no evil strong enough to take us down unless we bow to it.

You have been given the same authority that Jesus walked in upon this earth. Can you imagine for one moment that Jesus would cry himself to sleep at night because he could not control his fearful thoughts? Laughable! Do you believe he ever entertained thoughts of *"I'm just losing my mind,"* or *"I'm going to have a nervous breakdown?"* Let me tell you, if anyone ever had a reason to break down I think it would have been someone who had been beaten, ridiculed, stripped, spat upon and sent to walk down the center street of a city carrying a wooden cross upon mutilated shoulders. The pain itself, making no mention of the shame he so despised, would have broken most of us. Yet, he withstood the whole ordeal and maintained a sound mind. A mind that was still able to provide a covering for his mother after his death, a mind that still maintained its sharpness to the point of knowing when an eternal work had been finished.

We have been given the mind of Christ, my friend. Be strengthened by that knowledge. Be delivered in your mind this day. Say to the enemy, "I'm taking back what belongs to me." God has not given *you* a spirit of fear, but has given you abundant power, amazing love and a *sound mind*. Do not let yourself be deceived into thinking anything other than this truth.

Have you been struggling with any of the schemes we have talked about this week? If so, which ones?

_____
_____
_____
_____

Were you able to gain any ground in exposing his schemes and combating them?

_____
_____
_____
_____

What will you do next time you recognize one of these at work in your life?

_____
_____
_____
_____

Questions or comments concerning today's lesson:

CLASS NOTES

Week Seven

I Wish Someone Had Told Me
Falling Only Counts When You Do Not Get Up

"Who are you to judge someone else's servant? To his own master he stands or falls. And he will stand, for the Lord is able to make him stand."

Romans 14:4

Day 1
The Biggest Failures

Day 2
The Biggest Failures, cont.

Day 3
Beams and Splinters

Day 4
Letting Go

Day 5
Restoration

Sometimes the hardest thing in the world to do is admit that you have failed. It is embarrassing. It can be humiliating. It makes you feel like everyone is looking at you or talking about you. You just know that there is not one person who is not aware of how bad you messed up. Satan just loves it when you blow it. Why? Because you have separated yourself from God? No. Because he wants to try to convince you that you have. Your enemy takes great pleasure in playing our failure tapes. He turns up the volume on the big screen of our mind and plays it repeatedly. He taunts and tells us that we have really blown it this time. He sends discouragement and shame to bombard you and attempt to keep you out of the presence of God and His family here on earth. I have come to tell you,

"Even now my witness is in heaven; my advocate is on high."

Job 16:19

…and falling only counts when you do not get up!

Day 1

The Biggest Failures

Read the following passages then write your impression of what you have read.

I Samuel 16:11-13.
_____
_____
_____
_____

I Samuel 17:32-58.
_____
_____
_____
_____

I Samuel 18:5-7.
_____
_____
_____
_____

David really was something else, wasn't he? Brave, full of faith, talented, anointed of God. No wonder God had such tenderness toward him. There is much to be said about a man of valor!

Now, I would like you to look at another important passage concerning David's life.

Read II Samuel 11.

I think this is one of the saddest stories in the Bible. It is the account of the orchestrated betrayal and murder of an honorable man. Uriah the Hittite was a warrior, a servant in the armies of Israel. He was married to a woman he loved, and he was an obviously religious man. He was committed to his king and to the defense of his homeland. Verse 11 tells us that when David asked why Uriah did not go home, Uriah was incredulous that David could even make such a suggestion. "The ark of Judah and Israel are staying in tents…," he said, as if to say, "Are you crazy? I will not rest and be warm as long as the ark and my fellow warriors are not!" Uriah seemed to be a man of conviction and standards. He was fighting for his king. He must have been a loyal, brave man. Certainly, he was not a man who in any way deserved what would happen to him at the hand of David. Uriah spent his last nights sleeping on the cold ground in service to a man that would steal his wife and have him murdered.

I do not know about you, but somehow this passage of scripture does not describe to me, "A man after God's own heart." David broke most of the commandments of God in a very short period of time. He coveted, stole, committed adultery and murdered, not to mention the fact that his lust had become his god and he had placed it before obedience to his True God. How can this man, this *sinner*, possibly be the same man that was anointed by the prophet Samuel? The key lies in David's confrontation with his own sin. Many times we are confronted with our sin, only to walk away from it in rebellion. David's heart would not allow that. Let's take a closer look at the situation.

> *The LORD sent Nathan to David. When he came to him, he said, "There were two men in a certain town, one rich and the other poor. The rich man had a very large number of sheep and cattle, but the poor man had nothing except one little ewe lamb he had bought. He raised it, and it grew up with him and his children. It shared his food, drank from his cup and even slept in his arms. It was like a daughter to him.*
>
> *"Now a traveler came to the rich man, but the rich man refrained from taking one of his own sheep or cattle to prepare a meal for the traveler who had come to him. Instead, he took the ewe lamb that belonged to the poor man and prepared it for the one who had come to him."*
>
> *David burned with anger against the man and said to Nathan, "As surely as the LORD lives, the man who did this deserves to die! He must pay for that lamb four times over, because he did such a thing and had no pity."*
>
> *Then Nathan said to David, "You are the man! This is what the LORD, the God of Israel, says: 'I anointed you king over Israel, and I delivered you from the hand of Saul. I gave your master's house to you, and your master's wives into your arms. I gave you the house of Israel and Judah. And if all this had been too little, I would have given you even more. Why did you despise the word of the LORD by doing what is evil in his eyes? You struck down Uriah the Hittite with the sword and took his wife to be your own. You killed him with the sword of the Ammonites. Now, therefore, the sword will never depart from your house, because you despised me and took the wife of Uriah the Hittite to be your own.'*
>
> *"This is what the LORD says: 'Out of your own household I am going to bring calamity upon you. Before your very eyes I will take your wives and give them to one who is close to you, and he will lie with your wives in broad daylight. You did it in secret, but I will do this thing in broad daylight before all Israel.'"*
>
> *Then David said to Nathan, "I have sinned against the LORD."*
>
> *Nathan replied, "The LORD has taken away your sin. You are not going to die. But because by doing this you have made the enemies of the LORD show utter contempt, the son born to you will die."*
>
> *After Nathan had gone home, the LORD struck the child that Uriah's wife had borne to David, and he became ill. David pleaded with God for the child. He fasted and went into his house and*

spent the nights lying on the ground. The elders of his household stood beside him to get him up from the ground, but he refused, and he would not eat any food with them.
On the seventh day the child died. David's servants were afraid to tell him that the child was dead, for they thought, "While the child was still living, we spoke to David but he would not listen to us. How can we tell him the child is dead? He may do something desperate."
David noticed that his servants were whispering among themselves and he realized the child was dead.
"Is the child dead?" he asked.
"Yes," they replied, "he is dead."
Then David got up from the ground. After he had washed, put on lotions and changed his clothes, he went into the house of the LORD and worshiped. Then he went to his own house, and at his request they served him food, and he ate.
His servants asked him, "Why are you acting this way? While the child was alive, you fasted and wept, but now that the child is dead, you get up and eat!"
He answered, "While the child was still alive, I fasted and wept. I thought, 'Who knows? The LORD may be gracious to me and let the child live.' But now that he is dead, why should I fast? Can I bring him back again? I will go to him, but he will not return to me."
Then David comforted his wife Bathsheba, and he went to her and lay with her. She gave birth to a son, and they named him Solomon. The LORD loved him.

II Samuel 12:1-24

In II Samuel we see David confronted with his grave sin. When Nathan tells the story of the lamb, David is furious with the one who would do such a thing! Isn't it funny how easily we see the sins of others? Ponder that just a bit.

Questions or comments concerning today's lesson:

Day 2

The Biggest Failures…cont.

You may want to read over 2 Samuel 12 before going forward into today's lesson. We are going to pick up where we left off yesterday - right in the middle of David's fall.

In verse 5 of chapter 12, David declares that the man who did this must surely die. Unfortunately, it became David and Bathsheba's son who died for this sin. What do you think about the judgment meted out for this transgression?

_____
_____
_____

We are told in subsequent verses that David admitted his sin. Nathan then tells him that his sin is forgiven but there will be a penalty for the contempt brought upon the name of the Lord by his actions. David prays, fasts, cries out to God in his grief, and still the hand of the Lord is not stayed. His judgment is just as He had said – their son dies.

There are many who think that when they return to the Lord, confess their sins and receive forgiveness, the mess that they have made up until that point will simply vanish. Unfortunately, that is not the case. Sometimes we must walk our way out of sin's maze. If we walk out, we know how to get out should we ever find ourselves in a mess again. If we were instantaneously delivered, we would forever stray back into messes, never finding the strength to walk out by obedience and trust.

God delivers us on occasion, but it has been my experience that most of our deliverances are through obedience to God's commands and instruction.

We now see David faced with a decision. He has isolated himself to seek the mercy of the Lord concerning his son and has been refused. David could have very easily given up at that point. His lust had basically brought death and war into his household. He had murdered, committed adultery, lied, stolen and coveted, and in doing so, forfeited his son's life. He had a choice to make; would he go forward or stay in his grief.

Look back at verses 21-24. David picked himself up, dusted himself off, washed his face and asked for food. He was moving beyond his failure. He had asked the Lord to forgive him, pleaded for mercy, accepted the consequence of his sin, comforted those affected by his sin, then moved on.

We can learn much from David's example in this. Many of us have not gotten beyond our past sins.

We have confessed them – over and over and over - yet we never let go of them. Somehow, we have become convinced that while the blood of Jesus does cleanse others from their sin, our actions have gone beyond His ability to cleanse. When we try to let go of our past we hear the "Yes, but's…"- *"Yes, but you knew better. Yours was a knowing sin."* Alternatively, *"Yes, but you told God if He would forgive you that last time, you would never do it again."* Again, *"Yes, but do you really want to go back to God with that same old thing? I mean you're never really going to be free."* Then, there is probably one of the most painful of all, *"Yes, but you killed your own child when you had that abortion."*

In a very real sense, David was responsible for the death of his son. David's sin killed his son. The choice that David made brought it about. It was by his hand that death touched his son. Still, David would move beyond his sin and find forgiveness and release. I believe God is speaking to hearts right now and telling many that it is time to get up and move on. The penalty for your sin has been paid. Your tears and shame will not set you free. The shame He bore on the cross already has. You do not have to live in your past sins any longer.

As David did, you must get up from the ground, wash and perfume yourself, go to the house of the Lord and worship Him for His mercy and goodness, then eat and be refreshed.

Your God is a good and merciful God.

I would like us to look at David's Psalm of repentance. It should be a very familiar passage, but let's not allow that to keep us from finding the richness in the words.

> *Have mercy on me, O God, according to your unfailing love; according to your great compassion blot out my transgressions. Wash away all my iniquity and cleanse me from my sin. For I know my transgressions, and my sin is always before me.*
>
> *Against you, you only, have I sinned and done what is evil in your sight, so that you are proved right when you speak and justified when you judge. Surely I was sinful at birth, sinful from the time my mother conceived me. Surely you desire truth in the inner parts; you teach me wisdom in the inmost place.*
>
> *Cleanse me with hyssop, and I will be clean; wash me, and I will be whiter than snow. Let me hear joy and gladness; let the bones you have crushed rejoice. Hide your face from my sins and blot out all my iniquity.*
>
> *Create in me a pure heart, O God, and renew a steadfast spirit within me.*
>
> *Do not cast me from your presence or take your Holy Spirit from me. Restore to me the joy of your salvation and grant me a willing spirit, to sustain me. Then I will teach transgressors your ways, and sinners will turn back to you.*
>
> *Save me from bloodguilt, O God, the God who saves me, and my tongue will sing of your righteousness. O Lord, open my lips, and my mouth will declare your praise.*
>
> *You do not delight in sacrifice, or I would bring it; you do not take pleasure in burnt offerings. The sacrifices of God are a broken spirit;*
> *a broken and contrite heart, O God, you will not despise.*
>
> Psalm 51:1-17

I absolutely love this passage. It has been my prayer upon many occasions, moments when I simply could not find the words to express my grief over my constant failure. I have been comforted by the words pouring from the heart of this man. David had been entangled in his sin for at least nine months, more likely into his second year, without even showing remorse for his sin. Even longstanding sin that has been wallowed in for some time is still confrontation worthy and forgivable.

Nathan, a messenger sent from God, brought David's sin into the light. We must not despise the correction of the Lord. If you have been in sin for a while, there will be a confrontation of that sin if you wish to continue in the Lord. God is raising up Nathans that will speak the truth in love. He will give you the option of first listening to His voice, but know this; God will bring your sin to light should you fail to heed His instruction.

I know, I can hear it now, "What about mercy?" All I can say to that is,

"For the LORD your God is a consuming fire, a jealous God."

Dueteronomy 4:24

Many years ago I fell, and I fell *hard*. I had served the Lord all of my life but had become arrogant in my faith. The failures of others seemed so beyond my comprehension. I mean, I was a pillar, so why were they so weak? Anyway, this pillar crumbled and decided to blame God. When I finally returned home, having lived in the pigsty long enough, I had a conversation with God about what had happened. In this conversation I accused Him of having abandoned me. The poem you are about to read encompasses that conversation.

Restoration

How can I even begin, to share just what I feel?
How do I reach beyond the false veneer, to what is real?
To be laid out so openly, before my blinded eyes,
To strip away what others see , remove this old disguise.

What if I cannot find the heart that used to lie within?
What if there's no substance, no victory left to win?
What if I reach oh, so deep, and find true shallowness?
What if while trying to come clean, I make a bitter mess?

Somewhere beyond the faith to look, lies fear that longs to run,
From things best left in mind's recess, and deeds I'd wish undone.
Can past and present meet without true rending of the soul?
Can fragments, pieces, shreds and parts, when mended make a whole?

What am I looking for? Why must I undertake this quest?
Would not it be quite prudent, Lord, to let the sleeping rest?
"Yes, there are times, when pasts let go, forgotten ever be.
But there is a wall I'll not let stand between My child and Me.

You hide behind it, think I can't find it, and often shrink in fear,
But, I've come to tear it down, mirror before the face, sweet dear.
You fell away, yes, far away. You let me down, it's true.
Yet, through it all, My little one, My love still covered you.

I turned My face away, My pain was great for you, I wept,
For promises were broken and the vows you made weren't kept.
You broke before my very eyes, lay bruised and bloodied at my feet.
Though I longed to take you in my arms , destined appointments you did keep.

You turned your back, My hand went out, stayed judgment from your brow,
I turned and cried to angels close, "We'll help her soon, not now."
I had to let you go, My love, for your heart did leave Me first,
You hungered and turned not to Me, let others quench your thirst.

Unfaithful each and every deed, your heart hardened at My touch.
Through sleepless nights and deep soul fights, you threw away so much.
Into sin's lair, you fairly ran, so eager to be free,
"No," I called, "Please turn around, come running home to Me."

But, even as the words went past My lips, I knew them lost,
For your course was set, a journey started, there would be great cost.
You could not see it taking place, for your eyes were dark as night,
But in heavenlies above began the true and earnest fight.

You hang there in the balance, each side your soul desired,
But the prayers of those who loved you most, watered Satan's fire.
Scorched and singed you crawled to shore, your piercing cries did start,
But they came mere from your circumstance, not a true repentant heart.

Wounds sustained in private battle, not so apparent to the eye,
Still stand open, festered, bleeding at the wall 'tween you and I.
You do not trust Me to keep you sound, you fear I'll give you up,
You think there's no more water left, when I've a brimming cup.

You thirst for what you cannot find, hunger beyond your grasp,
While before you there's a table spread, and you have but to ask.
You're mad at Me, you feel I failed, when you needed Me most.
Yet, in your deepest desperation, I assure, there was a Host.

I never left you, never forgot the covenant we made,
When as a child, behind closed doors, My hand and heart I gave.
I loved you with the deepest love, your mind can't comprehend.
I promise you, I have not changed, same love now, as then.

Hurt and disappointment have followed your steps much,
But I've come to tell you daughter, I bring the gentle Master's touch.
It's time to come out now, dear one, the wall's just in the way.
You've no need to hide, come love, abide, in the Father's home today.

Be restored full and wholly, no settlement for less.
The battle's over, we have won, come through another test.
You think you failed this time, but you will come to understand,
As David did, when sin realized, You sought the Father's hand.

No, not for gain, or gifts longed for, child what you sought instead,
The touch of precious Shepherd's hand upon the sheep's small head.
Sweet comfort, sweet reunion, precious fellowship is found,
When chains are loosed, past cast away, and fettered hearts unbound.

I love you still.
Be free, in My name."

Questions or comments concerning today's lesson:

Day 3

Beams and Splinters

"Why do you look at the speck of sawdust in your brother's eye and pay no attention to the plank in your own eye? How can you say to your brother, 'Let me take the speck out of your eye,' when all the time there is a plank in your own eye?"

Matthew 7:3-4

I sat in one of the coolest Sunday school classes anywhere. Our teacher, Rodney, was sharing his heart in his usual off-the-wall way. He had (still has) a way of cutting through all of the garbage and making his point with creative impact. This particular day we had been discussing sin, redemption, judgment and mercy, all in regard to the family of Christ. As he began his teaching on mercy within the family, he opened with "Christians are the only two legged species that eat their wounded."

What followed was a wonderful teaching on restoration instead of judgment within the walls of the church. I still remember thinking, *'You know, he's right.'* I had grown up in a church where the slightest mistake could get you ostracized from church fellowship. This was a church where you dared not confess your sin for fear of being cast away from the rest of the body. Restoration was what you did to a house not a person. The bricks and mortar got a second chance – flesh and blood could just forget it. Never have I heard so many reasons given for fulfilling I Corinthians 5:5!

Just in case this is not a familiar passage, let me enlighten you:

"Hand this man over to Satan, so that the sinful nature may be destroyed and his spirit saved on the day of the Lord."

I Corinthians 5:5

While all scripture is God-breathed, I do not believe this mandate is applicable to all sin, just as Abraham's blessing of children as numerous as the sands of the sea is not applicable to every inhabitant of the earth. Picking and choosing scripture to meet our claim of the moment is a dangerous thing. I am a very human, flawed writer and I have a problem with people misquoting me. I cannot even begin to imagine how the God of the universe must feel when we play around with His absolute Truth. I digress…

I think now would be an excellent place to share one of my favorite scriptures. It has been a balm to me in times past:

"Brothers, if someone is caught in a sin, you who are spiritual should restore him gently."

Galatians 6:1

The extension of mercy, or the lack thereof in the body of Christ, is addressed in several ways throughout both the Old and New Testaments. Let's look at a few verses that tell us to be very careful how we deal with someone else's servant. Remember, we have been bought with a price and are not our own.

Matthew 18:21-35.

This is probably the most popular text on forgiving and restoring. Others speak to our response as Christians as well.

Luke 6:36, 37.

Matthew 7:1, 2.

Romans 14:4.

It is before his own master that he stands or falls. Trust me, I would rather fall before my Master than my fellow worker. I have done both, and my Master has always shown great compassion. My brothers and sisters have not always understood. It should not be so. We should be in agreement with the Father so that we may discern what is right and wrong, not sit in judgment. Judgment and discernment are two different things entirely. Check out the following passage. Take a moment and think about what you are reading.

> *"You judge by human standards; I pass judgment on no one. But if I do judge, my decisions are right, because I am not alone. I stand with the Father, who sent me. In your own Law it is written that the testimony of two men is valid. I am one who testifies for myself; my other witness is the Father, who sent me."*
>
> John 8:15-18

Agreement with the Father is not judgment. We were never intended to judge the hearts of men, but to discern what is good and evil. Remember, it is before a man's own master that he stands or falls.

The message of today's lesson was brought home to me the other afternoon when I went to pick my daughter up at school. When I arrived to pick her up, she was being escorted out by her teacher – not a good sign. Her teacher put her in the back seat and leaned in to speak with me. "Mrs. Loflin, we had a bit of a problem with our behavior today," she spoke as she cast a glance at my six-year-old in the back seat. "I'm sorry," I began. "What happened?" (It is always best to apologize before you even know what's coming - it softens them up!) "Well, on our field trip today, Katie kicked a little boy."

When we asked her why she had done it, she said another little girl had told her to. I turned in my seat to stare at the bent blonde head of my "Angel." Guilt was written all over her smudge-cheeked face. "Katie, why did you do that?" I demanded. "I don't know," came the simpering reply. "Well," the teacher continued, "I have taken away her smiley face stamp!" I almost laughed at the gravity with which she spoke those words of condemnation. "I will take away her smiley face too," I thought.

As the car pulled away, I began my *mother thing*. "Why, Katie? Why would you kick a little boy smaller than you?" Her response remained the same. "I don't know." I thought for a moment and changed my tactic. "Kaitlen, why was it wrong to kick that little boy?" The sniffles began as I awaited her reply. When the reply came, trust me, it was not what I expected. "Because he is someone else's little boy." My ears perked up to her answer. "What?" "Because he has a mommy somewhere who loves him and she is going to be very sad that I hurt him at school today." At that, tears began to stream down those guilty cheeks and they filled the corners of my eyes as well. I swallowed the lump in my throat as the Lord poured His loving correction through both my child and myself.

"Why is it wrong to treat your brother or sister in Christ that way?" "Because they are someone else's son or daughter. Because they have a Father who loves them very much, and He is going to be very sad that I hurt them today."

There are some of us who need to make things right with people we have sat in judgment on. If the Lord has brought anyone to mind as we have walked through today's lesson, write their names on the lines below and give a brief explanation of your failure to extend mercy.

_____
_____
_____
_____

Questions or comments concerning today's lesson:

Day 4

Letting Go

"But one thing I do: Forgetting what is behind and straining toward what is ahead."

Philippians 3:13

Read Matthew 11:28-30.

"Gentle and humble in heart." I love that. I love being loved by someone who is gentle and humble in heart. For many of us this description is far removed from anyone we have known in our lives. Most of the people we have known have had motives for doing the nice things they did. What a concept, someone who just wants to help you because He loves you, expecting nothing in return. We have a tendency to wait for the other shoe to drop. It's the "there has to be a catch" mentality we have come into as a society. But God, Love Incarnate, extends His hand, offers His shoulder, and says "Unload here. Lay your head down on my shoulder and tell me all about it." He invites us to climb into His lap and cry all of the tears we could possibly cry. He then dries our eyes and soothes us with His sweet voice. It is an encounter that takes away our heavy burdens and releases us from our worries.

So, what *is* the catch? We are treated as precious treasure, riches far beyond comprehensible value, and nothing is asked in return?

Yes, that is right.

Isaiah alluded to God's free gift.

> *"Come, all you who are thirsty, come to the waters; and you who have no money, come, buy and eat! Come, buy wine and milk without money and without cost."*

Isaiah 55:1

So, what is our part in all of this? We must *come*. We must *let him* do what He wants to do in our lives. God's gifts and mercy have been paid for. We need not pay for them a second time. God, however, will not force your hands and heart open and make you take the gift He is offering.

Sometimes it is hard to receive. There seems to be an obligation attached to receiving, and we definitely do not want to owe anyone anything. If I let you do something nice for me, then I am going to have to do something nice for you. Someone who already feels pressured to perform will feel a great deal of anxiety over this whole concept. Their concern is going to be about "what if my nice thing isn't as good as theirs?" Measuring up, even in doing what is good and benevolent, can become so stressful that people give up. They do not want you to help them and they are not going to help you. The pressure is gone, and all of a sudden so are friends and relationships. Giving and receiving keeps us in constant interaction with the body of Christ. This is not optional. It is a necessity for full-body-life. It is what families are about.

Now, comes the tricky part.

God does not *require* that we give to Him. He *desires* that we would receive from Him.

Does this make Him some great cookie jar in the sky? No! Most assuredly not. What He *gives* to us changes us in such a manner that we are compelled to give back to Him. You cannot receive an elaborate, extravagant gift and fail to say, *thank you*. It is an automatic response. Great kindness should always provoke great gratitude. If it does not, our hearts of stone definitely need to be turned into hearts of flesh.

Have you ever tried to dance while holding onto the doorframe? Doesn't work, does it? You have to let go to experience true freedom of movement. The same is true of God's dance of deliverance. If you are to experience true freedom of movement in the Spirit, you must let go. Release the doors you have hidden behind for so long, and allow yourself to walk out. Lay your past at His feet and do not pick it up again. Do not look back! Go forward. Set your eyes upon the face of your Beloved, listen to His beautiful voice singing sweet songs of love to you alone.

And dance!

Today's assignment (please choose to accept it):

Take 15 minutes today (more if you have it) and turn on your favorite music. Dance with Him. Let your spirit, soul and body be captivated by His presence. See Him smiling as you twirl about. You are His. He is yours. Take time in these moments to know that,

> *"The king is enthralled by your beauty;*
> *"honor him, for he is your lord."*

Psalm 45:11

Let it Go

You carry a wounded heart in hand,
You've done it now for years.
From time to time you take it out,
To mourn and shed your tears.

What should have healed so long ago,
Lays fresh and bleeding still,
For you refuse to lay it down,
Though oft you say you will.

Bound tight by cords of bitterness,
The pain a living thing,
It consumes your days, directs your ways,
Talons to mind, it clings.

Flashes from your past do play,
You long so to be free,
But, child, you cannot do alone,
What must be done by Me.

Only I can cleanse your mind,
Heal the scars you hide.
Daughter, lay all at My feet.
Forget all you have tried.

Complete and whole, My plan for you,
No ties to wounds of past.
Cease ups and downs, walk stable, sure,
For child, My healing lasts.

Still, one thing will I need of you.
Oh Yes, I'm sure you know.
If I'm to take the hurt away,
You must choose to let it go!

Questions or comments concerning today's lesson:

Day 5

Restoration

"If you are pure and upright, even now he will rouse himself on your behalf and restore you to your rightful place."

Job 8:6

This week we have talked about failures that come our way. We have discussed the fact that God is always ready to pick us up and bring us back into fellowship with Him. We have discussed forgiveness, and letting go of the past. We have determined to set our eyes upon our Savior and allow Him to lead us out of our messes and into His will. Having gone through all of this, I would now like to extend an even greater promise to you. He has promised to not only heal, forgive, refresh, seal, comfort and sustain you, but also to *restore* you. What a wonderful God we serve! In order to fully appreciate the impact of what I have just said, I think we need to look at what it means to be restored. We will then look at several scripture passages that extend this empowering promise of God.

Restore: apokathistemi (ap-ok-ath-is'-tay-mee); reconstitute (in health, home or organization): KJV - restore (again).

Restore: apokatallasso (ap-ok-at-al-las'-so); to reconcile fully: KJV - reconcile.

Restore: (Webster's) "to bring back to health or strength; to return anything taken away or lost."

Now that we fully understand what it means to be restored, let's look at our promised restoration. As you consider the following verses, I want you to think about whether or not you need restoration in the particular area mentioned. If you do, write "yes" and why in the space provided. If you are fully complete in the area, thank Him in the space provided.

_____
_____
_____

"And the God of all grace, who called you to his eternal glory in Christ, after you have suffered a little while, will himself restore you and make you strong, firm and steadfast."

I Peter 5:10

Do you need restoration of strength and steadfastness?

> *"I will strengthen the house of Judah and save the house of Joseph. I will restore them because I have compassion on them. They will be as though I had not rejected them, for I am the LORD their God and I will answer them."*
>
> Zechariah 10:6

Do you need to be restored in the area of your emotions? Have you walked in a lack of acceptance, a root of rejection?

> *"Restore us to yourself, O LORD, that we may return; renew our days as of old."*
>
> Lamentations 5:21

Have you ever walked closer to Him than you are at this moment? Do you have "Glory Days" with Him in your past that you long for?

> *"This is what the LORD says – your Redeemer, who formed you in the womb: I am the LORD, who has made all things, who alone stretched out the heavens, who spread out the earth by myself, who foils the signs of false prophets and makes fools of diviners, who overthrows the learning of the wise and turns it into nonsense, who carries out the words of his servants and fulfills the predictions of his messengers, who says of Jerusalem, 'It shall be inhabited,' of the towns of Judah, 'They shall be built,' and of their ruins, 'I will restore them.'*
>
> Isaiah 44:24-26

Before I ask you about your ruins, let me explain to you what they are. Ruins are damaged places; places that drain you and make you feel empty. Ruins may be places of downfall – places where you absolutely lost your faith and gave up. Now there is a weak, damaged area that must be restored (brought back to health). We all have ruins. Now is the time to let Him restore those places and heal you.

Do you have ruins? Place them before Him and ask Him to restore wholeness to those areas.

_____

_____

_____

_____

> *"Restore to me the joy of your salvation and grant me a willing spirit, to sustain me."*
>
> Psalm 51:12

What about your joy?

> *"The LORD will sustain him on his sickbed and restore him from his bed of illness."*
>
> Psalm 41:3

Are you sick in your body? What about your emotions? Have you been attacked in your flesh and now feel as if you have lost the battle?

_____
_____
_____

Now, if I have not given you a scripture that speaks to your personal need for restoration, allow me to give you one more.

> *"Repent, then, and turn to God, so that your sins may be wiped out, that times of refreshing may come from the Lord, and that he may send the Christ, who has been appointed for you - even Jesus. He must remain in heaven until the time comes for God to restore everything, as he promised long ago through his holy prophets."*
>
> Acts 3:19-21

Our God is a God of wholeness, healing, completeness. Anything less than this is not His will for you. You get do-overs and start-overs every day in this marvelous kingdom of God. Let Him do what He does best. Let Him love and restore you.

In the Bible study that I teach there is a wonderfully sweet woman. She has several children that keep her busy from sunup to sundown. I have never heard anything but good come out of her mouth. She is an encourager and a wonderfully humble spirit. So, I was truly touched when she shared with the class a dream the Lord had given her. I hope she will not mind if I share the heart of the dream. She had been standing before the Lord as He held a slate in His hand. She knew the slate was the one upon which her sins had been recorded. She watched as He lifted the slate and sent it crashing to the ground, shattering it. He then picked up a new slate.

He had chosen to break the slate and start with a new one because even when a board is erased there is a trace of what was written. There is *no trace* of our sin once it has been forgiven and cleansed through the blood of Jesus.

Questions or comments concerning today's lesson:

CLASS NOTES

Week Eight

I Wish Someone Had Told Me
It is Possible to Continually Know the Peace of God

"Let the peace of Christ rule in your hearts, since as members of one body you were called to peace."

Colossians 3:15

Day 1
When You Seek Me

Day 2
Peace like a River

Day 3
Entering His Rest

Day 4
The Whirlwind

Day 5
In That Day

Stressed out. How many times have you heard that phrase? How often do you experience it for yourself? You can see it on people's faces as you walk down the street, or even worse, when you are sitting in church on Sunday morning. The cares of this world chase us down and try to overtake us on a daily basis. We easily become consumed with worry and anxiety, our thought patterns becoming negative, robbing us of even the smallest victories. Let's face it. Small, human shoulders were never designed to carry weight of this magnitude. Oh, but there is a mighty arm upon which we may cast the burdens of this world, and this arm is mighty to save us. This arm is not short and it is extended with the offer of peace. The Word tells us in Ephesians, *"He, Himself is our peace."* Now, if we put that together with the scripture from Colossians 3:5, we begin to get a beautiful picture. We have been called to peace, and He is our peace. We have been called into fellowship with Christ and it is that fellowship that brings us into the peace of God. This week we will journey upon a well-traveled road in pursuit of the peace of God.

Day 1

When You Seek Me

"You will seek me and find me when you seek me with all your heart."

Jeremiah 29:13

Peace can be an elusive state. You want to attain it – to achieve it – but somehow it seems just beyond your grasp. It often falls into the category of "the grass is always greener." What do I mean? Well, everyone else seems to be walking in more peace than you are. I have one friend that seems to maintain her peace no matter what. The foundations of her faith have oft been shaken, yet I have found her to be peacefully stable. Her circumstances have cried chaos, still she has walked in the *"peace that passes all understanding."* It is because of this peace, a gift from God, that she has continued to be strengthened and to grow through adversity. Her secret? She knew His peace before the trials came and was able to keep it in the midst of them.

Too often we cry out for peace only as we find ourselves surrounded by flames of trial. How wise it would be to know the peace of God before the trial. Then we would not have to work to find it, but would be able to rest, never having left it.

Today I would like to look at wholehearted pursuit of peace.

Read Psalm 34:14.

"Whoever would love life and see good days must keep his tongue from evil and his lips from deceitful speech. He must turn from evil and do good; he must seek peace and pursue it."

I Peter 3:10, 11

Please Read Ephesians 2 and answer the following questions.

Verse 1 tells us that we were _____ in our transgressions and sins as we <v.2> followed the ways of the _____ of the kingdom of the air. This is the same spirit that is at work in the sons of _____. v.3>All of us also lived among them at one time, _____ the _____ of our sinful nature and following its _____ and _____. Like the rest, we were _____ _____ objects of wrath.

We had no peace at this time. Those who are lost in their sins, running from fleshly demand to fleshly demand, have no peace. Their lives are spent in pursuit of the next fix, the next thrill, the next feel good medication that will make them forget, if only for a moment, that there is no peace in their lives. No matter what they try, they will not find the peace they seek, for to find that peace they must first find Him. Finding Him is one of life's greatest paradoxes. For, while we are looking for Him, He has been in pursuit of us throughout eternity. We are searching for someone who has longed to capture us all along.

Religion is man's pursuit of God. Redemption is God's pursuit of man.

Religion would dictate that in order to truly find God you must behave in a way that God might find acceptable. You must *deserve* to be called His, or *earn* the title, so to speak. Redemption simply says,

> *"I am my Beloved's and He is truly mine."*
>
> Song of Solomon 6:3

What has this to do with peace? You will only find true peace when you believe that you are found in the Beloved. When you can finally accept that Someone loves you completely, just as you are – flaws and all – you cease having to work so hard at being acceptable. Your heart is set free from the constant struggles with imperfection as you set your eyes on Perfection Himself. Because He is perfect, you do not have to be. Because His love is complete, you too can be. All of the empty places you have tried to fill with performance are suddenly filled with pure acceptance, no strings attached.

Acceptance is a concept so foreign to many of us that we find it quite difficult to grasp. How can someone possibly love us so much that he or she does not see the glaringly transparent flaws (Mine seem to be neon signs, at times.)? How can someone love us that much? I honestly do not understand it myself. I just believe it. I know that it is true, just because He told me so.

> *"The LORD appeared to us in the past, saying: "I have loved you with an everlasting love."*
>
> Jeremiah 31:3

> *"But from everlasting to everlasting the Lord's love is with those who fear Him, and his righteousness with their children's children."*
>
> Psalm 103:17

Finding peace is about finding the love of God. Knowing that you are in right standing with God, no matter what may come your way, is a rest for your spirit, soul and body. Surety of your salvation is a healing balm to a struggling soul. We can find peace when we seek Him with our whole heart.

> *"And without faith it is impossible to please God, because anyone who comes to him must believe that he exists and that he rewards those who earnestly seek him."*
>
> Hebrews 11:6

Righteousness, *peace* and joy in the Holy Ghost. This is the reward of all who dwell in the Kingdom of the Father. Don't you think it is about time you possessed the kingdom?

Do you believe it is possible to know the peace of God at all times?

It is Possible to Continually Know the Peace of God

When was the last time you truly rested in your spirit?
_____

Do you believe that it is God's will for you to live without worry and anxiety?
_____

How do you think He intends for us to *enter into His rest*?
_____
_____
_____
_____

If you had to bring it down to one year, what would have been your most anxiety-filled period of time, and why?
_____
_____
_____
_____

During that time were you relying heavily upon the Lord, or did you turn from Him to your circumstances?
_____
_____
_____
_____

Looking back, what might you do differently if you were faced with the same situation today?
_____
_____
_____
_____

Remember:

Peace is not a thing attained or state to be achieved.
Peace is but a knowing that His Word can be believed

Questions or comments concerning today's lesson:

Day 2

Peace Like a River

"If only you had paid attention to my commands, your peace would have been like a river, your righteousness like the waves of the sea."

Isaiah 48:18

If you had only paid attention…If you had only paid attention…If you had only paid attention!

How many times have we heard that before? Well, maybe you haven't heard it as many times as I have (I can be quite headstrong when left to my own devices), but I am sure you have heard it at some point. Maybe a teacher had to prod you out of your daydream with a "Well, what do you think about that, Johnny?" or your mother peered into your bomb shelter of a room and said "you obviously were not paying attention when I said *clean* your room." This is an admonition, a correction, a calling to attention. "If you had paid attention, this would not have happened." I think my mom could have definitely used that one against me when I ran her car through a fence while trying to drive with a poodle on my lap, but I digress.

Paying attention. Sounds like something you owe, right? If you owe something, you pay it. *Attention* was the price to be paid for attaining *peace like a river*. Small price for something of so great a value, don't you think? God is in essence saying "I have a present for you; all you have to do is pay attention to how I tell you to use it. It's a free gift, but there are instructions that go with it." We, in turn, say, "Give me the gift, I can figure it out on my own." It is that attitude that has led to many disasters, wouldn't you say? It is our lack of attention to detail that leads us to build unicycles with extra parts, when what we wanted was a tricycle. God has given us a manual with which we may fully utilize all of the wonderful blessings, talents, fruits and gifts He has given us, but our tendency is to play with the gifts, never using them the way He intended.

We want peace because we think it will make us calm and relaxed. Peace does not calm us, but makes us strong enough to walk forward when our knees are shaking. It strengthens the resolve of our Spirit.

When Isaiah wrote the words *"If only you had paid attention to my commands, your peace would have been like a river, your righteousness like the waves of the sea,"* you can almost feel the compassion in the heart of the God inspired rebuke. "Don't you see what I am offering you?" He seems to be saying. It reminds me of Jesus' poignant words as He overlooked Jerusalem.

"O Jerusalem, Jerusalem…how often I have longed to gather your children together, as a hen gathers her chicks under her wings, but you were not willing!"

Luke 13:34

There is a plea for us to accept His goodness. What a ridiculous situation! We go around begging God for crumbs and turn from the full inheritance of an heir to the King of Glory. Our understanding has been darkened by our carnality and we no longer see the truth of all that our relationship with God affords us.

Peace like a river belongs to you as you obey His commands. Righteousness as the waves of the sea will rest upon you as you walk in His precepts. The divine laws of the universe are set into motion when you come in line with His will for you. What is His will? That you believe! That you believe Him when He says that peace is yours.

> *"Peace I leave with you; my peace I give you. I do not give to you as the world gives. Do not let your hearts be troubled and do not be afraid."*
>
> John 14:27

Hope is yours.

> *"And again, Isaiah says, "The Root of Jesse will spring up, one who will arise to rule over the nations; the Gentiles will hope in him. May the God of hope fill you with all joy and peace as you trust in him, so that you may overflow with hope by the power of the Holy Spirit."*
>
> Romans 15:12-13

Understanding and enlightenment are yours.

> *"I pray also that the eyes of your heart may be enlightened in order that you may know the hope to which he has called you, the riches of his glorious inheritance in the saints."*
>
> Ephesians 1:18

Peace like a river…like a river.

What is a river like? It is constantly changing and moving. It turns corners and rounds bends. It tumbles over rocks and through tight crevices. It rushes and becomes most forceful when the path is obstructed. It fights against restraint. A river brings life and nourishment. It touches the lives of all who come near it. A river is full of power, strength and commitment to the course. But, most importantly, a river must always flow from a source. It is not self-sustaining. Remove the inflow from the source and the river will inevitably dry up.

The same holds true for your supply of peace. There will be times when it is so strong you can face any obstacle. At other times, it will seem to flow quietly through your spirit. Whatever curve the day may bring, whatever bend you may be surprised by, the river will remain strong enough to take you through it as long as the source is flowing freely. God did not use the word *river* by mistake. Peace like a stream or peace like a trickle does not have the impact that *river* carries. God said *river* because He meant *river*.

If your river has been flowing like a stream, maybe even become stagnant for lack of fresh water, let me encourage you to unblock your source. How? Begin to obey His commands again. If He has asked you to do something you have not done yet, do it! Begin to listen for His voice and do what He tells you to do. Stem by stem, branch by branch, the dam of disobedience will be destroyed and your peace will flow like a river over your parched spiritual lands.

God's plan for you is peace. If you do not believe me, just ask Him. He is waiting for the opportunity to truly flood your soul.

The River

Take me Father, to the place
Where peace does plot its course
Where rivers of contentment surge
And faith does find its source.

Take me to the very edge
Where waterfalls do flow
Deep into the wells of grace
Where valiant men dare go.

Take me deeper, let me see
The full breadth of this span
Show me, as the waters churn
I'm resting in Your plan.

Questions or comments concerning today's lesson:

Day 3

Entering His Rest

"There remains, then, a Sabbath-rest for the people of God; for anyone who enters God's rest also rests from his own work, just as God did from his."

Hebrews 4:9, 10

You walk into the house after a long day, the air is cool and the roast that you put in the crock-pot that morning sends a wonderful aroma to tease your senses. You step out of your heels and your feet sink into the carpet as you drop your purse onto the table. You tilt your heard forward and lift your hands to massage the sore muscles in the back of your neck. As you straighten, your eyes scan the living room and you see that your workday has only begun, there is still much to be attended to. But, then your eyes fall on the big soft recliner and you have a decision to make.

Recliner. Work. Recliner. Work.

You look around again at all that has to be done. You really want to just sit down for a moment and close your eyes and put your feet up, but you know the work will not get done if you do not do it. You think about it for just another moment; and you sigh as you begin to pick up the mess someone else has left for you to clean.

Sometimes it is okay to choose the recliner.

What made you choose the labor over the rest? Was it a sincere desire to be done with the mess, or was it a sense of guilt that someone might see the mess? Maybe it was fear that someone might blame you for the mess? Your answer is telling.

If you truly wanted to get rid of the mess – great! God is going to help all of us who truly want the messes out of our lives. Our motivation for doing the things we do is quite important to Him. If you are just afraid that someone will see the mess and you will be embarrassed, more than likely you are driven by a desire to please others that can, if not dealt with, lead to bondages in the area of trying to please man instead of God.

If you are afraid of getting in trouble because of the mess, you are probably walking on eggshells that should never have been put in your path. Fear should *not* be your motivator. The only fear we are to have is *"the fear of the Lord – which is the beginning of wisdom."*

Okay, before anyone goes running off to tell their husband I said you did not have to ever clean the house again, let me just clarify a couple of things.

We have responsibilities and commitments to our families that require that we take care of their primary, basic needs; food, shelter and love. Food requires that meals be prepared and grocery shopping be done. Shelter needs to be clean and safe, and love should be expansive and easily expressed. The rest of it… Well, the rest of… The rest…

Ah, yes, the *rest*. We get that too, ya know. It is okay to sit down and kick your feet up for a while. Take your hair down, mess it up with your fingers, slide on some sweats and wash your make-up off. Grab your thickest scrunch socks and a good book and veg-out. It is good for you. You need to take a break *sometimes*. You do not have to feel guilty about relaxing and taking it easy *on occasion*. Notice I said *on occasion*, not all of the time.

By the same token, there are times when we come into His presence we must *choose the recliner*. There are times when we must cease our perpetual motion and *be still*.

Too often Christians think they have backslidden if they are not doing something. Well, my friend, resting *is* doing something. It is quieting your spirit before the Lord and allowing Him to speak to you in a way that you could not hear when you were bustling about. Just as your body needs to rest, so does your spirit. It must have times of refreshing and renewal. Many times, in charismatic circles, we equate revival and jubilation with refreshing and renewal. They are entirely different things. I am refreshed and renewed physically when I climb out of a hot bubble bath after having soaked for an hour. I am neither revived nor jubilated during that time. Being refreshed required little more than allowing myself to rest in the warmth of the water. Something was given back to me and I came out better than when I went in. Why? Because I just took the time to rest.

Many of us need to learn to do that in the spirit.

It has been a long day. You walk into His house, the air is fresh and the Bread of Presence calls to your senses. You step out of your shoes, your feet coming in contact with Holy Ground as your tip your head forward in abjection. Your hands come up and you feel the tension ease from your body. You open your eyes and see the mess you have made of the day. You know that you have to clean it up. Your gaze falls upon a beautiful mercy seat. You long so to just enter in and rest upon that beautiful seat – to close your eyes and let the day wash away. Still, there is much to be done if you are going to get the mess cleaned up.

Rest. Work. Rest. Work.

May we say with John,

> *"We set our hearts at rest in His presence."*

I John 3:19

> *"Let the beloved of the LORD rest secure in him, for he shields him all day long, and the one the LORD loves rests between his shoulders."*

Deuteronomy 33:12

I want you to know that there is forgiveness for the sinner. There is strength for the weak. There is hope for the hopeless and help for the helpless. There is a time to work. And yes, there is a time to rest.

"This is the resting place, let the weary rest;"

Isaiah 28:12

It is okay. You have permission to take a load off.

"Come to me all you who are weary, and I will give you rest."

Matthew 11:28

I would like you to write a prayer asking God to show you how to rest in Him. Make a commitment to *enter into His rest*.

_____
_____
_____
_____
_____

Questions or comments concerning today's lesson:

Day 4

The Whirlwind

"No sooner are they planted, no sooner are they sown, no sooner do they take root in the ground, than he blows on them and they wither, and a whirlwind sweeps them away like chaff."

Isaiah 40:24

Have you ever felt like you were in the middle of a whirlwind? Your circumstances seem to wrap around you and overtake you. The sound of the storm increases to such a fevered pitch that you can see or hear nothing beyond what is right in front of you. Panic claws at your heart and your breathing seems labored. You want out, but you see no way through the torrent that rages all around you. You are looking for daylight but it is obscured by the whirlwind of debris. Before you lose heart and faint, look up!

If you are standing in the middle of a whirlwind, the only way you can see beyond the storm is to look up. When you look up you will see the beauty of the heavens. You will see the sun breaking through and shining on a world that you cannot even see from your vantage point. There is life outside the storm you are living in. In order to see it – and gain perspective – you have to stop trying to see your way out through the storm, and look, instead, to the Master of the wind.

When you look up your entire perspective is changed. I have done it repeatedly in my own life. I become so focused on the whirlwind that is trying to wreak havoc in my life, that I lose sight of God, who is able to calm the winds. However, if we can come to realize the *work* of the whirlwind, maybe we can lose some of our fear of it.

Just as a fire consumes everything in its path, yet leaves residue that is conducive to abundant new growth; so does the whirlwind leave something of benefit behind: Things unshakable and abundant space for the new. Everything that does not have a firm foundation will be shaken and taken down in a whirlwind, but when the rubble has been cleared away you get to start over. The only problem is that we sometimes stand in the rubble for a really long time, not sure what we are going to do with the mess, and blame God for letting it happen in the first place. Our job is to clear away the rubble – just let it go, burn it up, then get on with the process of rebuilding on a firm foundation.

Let's look at a couple of scriptures that give us instruction about allowing ourselves to be shaken. What does God think about our lives being in a mess and what can we do to avoid it?

1. Look up! Change your perspective. Get your eyes off the whirlwind and onto your Father.

"I have set the LORD always before me. Because he is at my right hand, I will not be shaken."

Psalm 16:8

Have you ever been in a crowded airport waiting for someone's flight to come in? It is usually quite chaotic. Lots of people, lots of noise. It can be very distracting. But when the plane lands and the passengers begin to disembark, you become quite focused because you are looking for the face of your loved one. Everything around you fades as you scan the crowd for the one you long to see. Finally, you see them. As far as you are concerned, the rest of the mess is just background noise, for you have found what and who you are looking for.

We should be the same when facing the chaos of the storm. Look for His face. Let the rest of the world become background music to the dance that you are going to dance with your Beloved.

2. Run to your shelter.

"He alone is my rock and my salvation; he is my fortress, I will never be shaken."

Psalm 62:2

Turn to the 91st Psalm and fill in the blanks.

"He who _____ in the _____ of the Most High will _____ in the shadow of the Almighty. I will say of the LORD, "He is my _____ and my _____, my God, in whom I trust." Surely, he will _____ you from the fowler's snare and from the deadly pestilence. He will _____ _____ with his feathers, and under his wings you will find _____; his faithfulness will be your shield and rampart. You will not _____ the terror of night, nor the arrow that flies by day, nor the _____ that stalks in the darkness, nor the_____ that destroys at midday. A thousand may fall at your side, ten thousand at your right hand, but it _____ _____ come near you."

Psalm 91:1-7

You have a shelter from the storm. Set your eyes on Him and run toward Him. He is your safety. He will be your peace until the whirlwind passes.

There is, however, a shaking that comes from Him; a trying of our foundations. He is making sure that the place we are standing is secure. When the storm comes by His hand, please know that He is still your shelter and in the midst of the shaking it must be to Him alone that you cling. He is your Father and He always knows what is best for you. He will help you rid your life of that which is of no value and has no strength. God is preparing the Bride to be clothed in strength so that He may present her to His Son on that appointed day.

"She is clothed with strength and dignity; she can laugh at the days to come."

Proverbs 31:25

> *"At that time his voice shook the earth, but now he has promised, 'Once more I will shake not only the earth but also the heavens.' The words "once more" indicate the removing of what can be shaken – that is, created things – so that what cannot be shaken may remain. Therefore, since we are receiving a kingdom that cannot be shaken, let us be thankful, and so worship God acceptably with reverence and awe, for our "God is a consuming fire."*
>
> Hebrews 12:26-29

It will take a strong bride to walk alongside one such as this.

Know that the whirlwind quickly passes. You may feel consumed by the storm at this moment, but the walls of wind are not as thick as you might think. Soon, they will begin to dissipate and your path will open up before you once again.

> *"As the whirlwind passeth, so is the wicked no more: but the righteous is an everlasting foundation."*
>
> Proverbs 10:25 (KJV)

He is our everlasting foundation. When we are found in Him, we are clothed with strength and dignity - whirlwind or no whirlwind!

The following poem is for those who feel like the strong winds have left you struggling to hold on to the ledge.

Barely Hangin' On

Walk on by. Walk on by,
Forget me on this ledge so high,
Desperation, sound your sigh,
I'm barely hangin' on.

Hands are bleeding. Wrists are sore,
I try to hold a little more,
Fingertips slide 'cross the floor,
I'm barely hangin on.

Crying once, calling twice,
Who will pay this torments price?
None but One sure will suffice,
I'm barely hangin on.

Must be blind, don't see me here,
Footsteps sound, so many near,
My hands are trampled, cries they can't hear,
I'm barely hangin' on.

Desperate now, can't do a thing,
Come gentle wind of mighty wings,
Lovers' voice so sweetly sings,
She's barely hangin' on.

Swiftly! Swiftly! Bring to Me,
My small ones falling, can't you see?
I'll hold her close now. My child can't be,
Barely hangin' on.

Questions or comments concerning today's lesson:

Day 5

In That Day

"In that day you will say: "I will praise you, O LORD. Although you were angry with me, your anger has turned away and you have comforted me."

Isaiah 12:1

Today we will talk about the peace of completion. Peace that comes when the battle is over and the work has been finished. We will talk about the peace that you know when you have done all that you can do and you are instructed to just stand in that place and have faith. We will talk about comforting, sustaining, strengthening peace. A peace that completes us as nothing else can. *"For He Himself is our peace."*

I remember when I was a young mother, probably in my early 20's, I had the most vivid dream. I dreamt I was standing in the middle of my living room doing battle with the forces of darkness that were trying to invade my home. This particular night the dream seemed so very real, I could see the demons of all shapes and sizes trying to come into my house. They were pressing their faces to the windows, clawing at the screen door and pounding on the walls and roof. Instead of being terrified, I began to battle. I would turn to one and pray in my spirit and it would fall away. Then I would turn to the next and fight with the Word. I turned and spun, turned and spun; spoke the word and spoke the word; I prayed and fought and prayed some more. I was so exhausted. I remember thinking 'there is just no way!' But, I continued to fight.

All through the night I stood guard in my dream, until at last, the dawn broke and the last of the attackers had been thwarted. When the last one fell, I awoke. The sun was streaming through the bedroom window, another day laid ahead – one full of babies and diapers and constant running – and I was more tired than I had ever been in my life. I literally could not lift my head off the pillow.

Looking back, I can see so many lessons taught in that eight-hour period, but the one that stands out at this moment is the fact that I was exhausted because I had fought alone. Not once during that battle do I remember asking God to help me. I had used His name, even used His Word, but I did not let Him fight for me. The battle would have been quickly won had I but asked Him to fight for me. I know that He was just waiting for the invitation to join in the battle.

Yes, I believe that we have to stand and fight for ground, but I do not believe the results of the battle can be borne by shoulders the size of ours. God alone knows how to defeat the Liar from the word go. My eight-hour ordeal could have been settled at one blast from the consuming fire that is our

God. I could have rested long before I did had I allowed the Mighty Warrior to fight for me.

I did not know then that the battle belonged to the Lord. I thought He required me to fight to the point of exhaustion before He would step in and take over. I now know that He was just waiting for me to get out of the way!

What has this to do with *In That Day*? A day is coming when only those who allow Him to fight on their behalf will be able to make it through the battles they will be faced with. It is only through complete and total reliance on Him that we will be able to stand against our adversary, the Devil. He is waging war as he has never waged war before because he knows his time is short. Our peace is in resting in the arms of the Warrior. Does this mean we do nothing? No. It means we do what He says to do, even if what He asks is difficult.

He fights – we stay close. I love that!

What about all of you who have been fighting so long you cannot even remember when the battle began and what it is about? It is time to move in close to the Warrior. It is time to let One Who is battle tested take over. It is time to concede that you are weak and let One Stronger step in. It is time to get out of His way and let Him fight the battle that belongs to Him.

It is time to pursue the peace of your spirit.

Many are still fighting battles that have been won. It is like shouting *get out!* to an empty room. It is already done. Warfare can become a mindset if you let it. Even as I say that, I know that there will be many who think that they must maintain a warfare mindset. But, remember what the Word says:

> *"Set your minds on things above, not on earthly things. For you died, and your life is now hidden with Christ in God."*
>
> Colossians 3:2, 3

Now, before all of you who are really into spiritual warfare begin to fight against what I am saying, let me say that I know there is a battle going on and that we are involved. I know that the forces of darkness are battling the forces of light even as we speak. I am also aware, however, that all troops get *shore leave* of one sort or another. Fresh troops are sent in when battle-worn troops need a break. Yes, you will go back into battle – you never know when the call may come – but it is okay to regroup occasionally and let your spirit rest.

If you are worn out from the battle, let yourself fall into the peace of God.

> *"He makes me lie down in green pastures; he leads me beside quiet waters, He restores my soul."*
>
> Psalm 23:2

Does this sound like a battlefield to you? I do not think so. What could God have been thinking here? No battlefield, just green pastures. Lie down in green pastures! Quiet waters! *What do you mean? How do I rebuke a stream or fight against restoration of my soul? Do you really want me to rest from the battle?* That makes it sound like He restores me when I lie down and get quiet. *How can that be true when my life is spent in the battle? Is it true that I can actually rest from the constant warfare?*

Oh, yes. It can be and most definitely is true.

> *"I myself will tend my sheep and have them lie down, declares the Sovereign LORD."*
>
> Ezekiel 34:15

A day is coming when the Lamb will lie down with the Lion, when the battles will cease and the victor will lead a train of vanquished foes. There is coming a day of rest for the weary, a peace for the battle-worn. There comes a day unlike any other; a day when struggle gives way to peace!

> *"In that day I will make a covenant for them with the beasts of the field and the birds of the air and the creatures that move along the ground. Bow and sword and battle I will abolish from the land, so that all may lie down in safety. I will betroth you to me forever; I will betroth you in righteousness and justice, in love and compassion. I will betroth you in faithfulness, and you will acknowledge the LORD.*
> *"In that day..."*
>
> Hosea 2:18-20

Yes. In that day we may lie down in safety. Lord, hasten the day!

What battle(s) do you need to rest from?

_____
_____
_____
_____

How long have you been fighting without rest?

_____
_____
_____
_____

Do you know what started the battle – what seed might have been planted to produce a harvest of war?

_____
_____
_____
_____

It may not be everyone's time of rest. Only you and the Lord know where you stand in this battle. If He is telling you to dig in and fight, ask Him to fight with you. If He is telling you to rest, just say *Yes, Lord,* and lie down at His feet. Know that your time of rest should bring refreshing. Watch for signs of your renewal – feel the strength entering your spirit as you commune with your Father. When you feel the strength flow from Him into your being, stand and enter the battle as He bids. Even the mightiest of warriors must trust their leader, for it is His experience that will carry you through…

Until that day.

Questions or comments concerning today's lesson:

CLASS NOTES

Week 9

I Wish Someone Had Told Me God is my Only Constant

For Jesus doesn't change--yesterday, today, tomorrow, he's always totally himself.
                                                    Hebrews 13:8 (Message)

Day 1
Changing Times

Day 2
Changing Seasons

Day 3
Changing Plans

Day 4
Changing Relationships

Day 5
Changing Heart

I am learning to expect the unexpected. I am constantly amazed by the changes going on around me. Just when I think I have everything all figured out – *Wham!* All of the rules have changed. Not only the rules, but my husband, my children, my job, my likes and dislikes, strengths and weaknesses, even my dreams and goals have changed. With everything spinning around as it does, we must have a focal point. One who does not change like shifting shadows. We must know where we begin and where we end. God alone is our constant. He does not change. You can count on Him to be the same "*yesterday, today and forever.*"

When the changes come, roll with them - straight into the arms of your Rock!

Day 1

Changing Times

"When times are good, be happy; but when times are bad, consider: God has made the one as well as the other."

Ecclesiastes 7:14

Today, I would like you to take a little extra time for your lesson. We are going to take a trip back into your childhood and then into your teen years. We will then bring things forward to this point and time. I know, it sounds like we may need a psychiatric couch for this, but I feel sure that we can handle it.

Try to remember the world you lived in when you were ten. I doubt you will remember news stories or anything like that, but I want your impression of the state of your world back then. Was it safe? How did you spend your day? What kind of neighborhood did you live in? Who was your best friend? What did you like to do? How were evenings spent in your home? What was your mother like? What about your dad? What was your biggest worry at that time?

_____
_____
_____
_____

Now, what about when you were 16? Had anything changed in your home? You can probably remember some of the big events going on in the world at that time. Who was your best friend? What did you like most about high school? What did you least enjoy about that time in your life? What was your favorite pastime? What was your biggest worry at that time? Was this a good or bad time in your life?

_____
_____
_____
_____

Okay, we can bring it home now. Do you feel safe in the world today? What is your biggest worry or concern? Who is your best friend? How are your evenings spent? What is your favorite thing to do? How often do you get to do that favorite thing? What is the best part of your life right now?

What is the worst part? If you could wake up in the morning and change three things, what would they be?

1. _____
2. _____
3. _____

Why are we doing this today? Because I want to show you that no matter what is going on in your life, it is still your life. I realize that this sounds really strange, but I want you to take ownership of every part of your life; the good, the bad and all of the in-between. Everything that has taken place in your life has only served to make you the person that you are today, and the person that you are is well-loved by God.

Your scars are roadmaps that lead others toward right paths. Your wounds are milestones alongside roads leading toward personal victories. Your failures are signposts that point others toward Him and your tears clearly define the well-trod trails of perseverance.

Be proud of what Christ has wrought out of years long past. The only years that are wasted years are the ones you did not thank God for bringing you through.

When I was a child, I thought I would never get out of the country - not the U.S.; the hollow. Many of my days were spent wondering what it would be like to live in the city. I wanted a big house and fancy clothes. I wanted to be somebody special – not just a little redheaded, freckled faced tom-girl from the sticks.

Looking back, I see how blessed my life truly was. I had a mother who poured her life into me and taught me everything I would ever need to be a whole person. I had four sisters who alternately harassed then fought for me. I was an award-winning athlete, third in my class academically and had more friends than I knew what to do with. My life was good, yet I wanted more. I was quite greedy and wanted what I did not have. I longed to climb over the fence and grab some of that greener grass. I find it quite ironic, however, that now possessing the greener grass I so longed for as a child, I find myself longing instead for the gently rolling hills and country breezes that swept through our little hollow.

If I could, I would take my children back to those same dirt roads and raise them in the same unassuming manner in which I was raised. The grass is now much greener on those childish footpaths long forsaken.

What is my point? Just that our lives are forever changing, and there is beauty to be found in every day that we live. The things you long for today will not be what you expect, and the things you were not even looking for will be the bright points of your life. I once read a quote, which read, "Life is what happens while you are waiting on the big stuff."

It is so true! My youth was spent wanting to be a teenager. My teen years were spent longing to be an adult. My adult years are spent in pursuit of…something - it changes from day to day. But somewhere in the middle of all of the pursuits, our lives are changing and passing us by. We *"chase the wind, and reap the whirlwind."* It all passes away before we realize what has happened.

Change only proves one thing - you are still alive! Enjoy today. You are not promised tomorrow.

Assignment:

Buy yourself some flowers today (or pick them if you have access). Put them on your kitchen table and stop to enjoy them every time you walk through the room.

Questions or comments concerning today's lesson:

Day 2

Changing Seasons

"He changes times and seasons; he sets up kings and deposes them. He gives wisdom to the wise and knowledge to the discerning."

Daniel 2:21

I once wrote a song entitled "**Seasons Change**."

I was going through a change of seasons in my life (we'll call it that because it sounds much better than saying my life was falling apart), and I became very focused on the fact that I was no longer a child and now had responsibilities that seemed to overwhelm me.

I had two young children who thought I was actually supposed to know what I was doing, and a husband who had moved us six hours away from my mama and sisters. The First Gulf War was in full swing and I was in a full-blown panic. My emotions took over and I became an unbelievable mess. I really let Satan do a number on me and by the time he was through, I literally felt like I was having a breakdown.

I remember my husband coming home from work one evening and finding me crying in the bedroom. When he asked me what was wrong, I, of course, could not put it into words (only a woman truly understands what I mean), but he kept pushing until it finally all came tumbling out something like this: "I was watching and Saddam Hussein is going to blow everything up and there is a fault-line that runs across this area of the country and they predicted an earthquake, and Matthew is never going to have any hair because Aaron's teacher pinched his arm and the vacuum cleaner had smoke coming out of it and there's no money for anything and the world must be coming to an end because long-distance phone calls to my mom just make me miss her too much."

My poor husband just looked at me for a moment, and with all of the compassion of a grizzly bear said, "If you don't straighten up I'm sending you to your mother!"

What he did not understand was that at that particular moment, I wanted nothing more than to be with my mother. He thought he was making a threat, I thought he was dangling a carrot in front of me. It makes me laugh now. It made me mad then.

I was cracking up and he did not know how to handle me. The leaves were falling off my tree, a season of my life was fading away, and I did not know what to do. I had come face to face with the fact that I was a grown up mommy who had somehow found herself in the middle of a life she had not planned for. I needed help. I needed someone to lead me through a difficult time until I could have my feet firmly planted in that new season. I needed my Strong Father to take care of his little girl. He did. I made it through that change of season, breaking branches and all. God was with me. He sustained me.

Read Psalm 55:22.

Have you ever found yourself in the middle of a season crisis you did not see coming? If so, when? What did you do to get through it?

_____
_____
_____
_____

Some of you may be right in the middle of a change now. Too often, we think that the only real change we go through is biological and occurs in our mid to late fifties. Wrong! We are constantly going through changes. New mom, school days, teen years, college, empty nests, grandchildren; our seasons are marked by the lines that appear on our once unlined brow. Like the rings of a tree, each line tells a story of a season past. Good times, bad times - they are all there, etched upon paths soon to be trod by our own daughters. They too will see many seasons come and go, and it is our job as Christian women to see that they face these paths with wisdom, grace and strength. We must point them to their Strong Father so that they may run to Him when they need sustenance. I remember four such little girls; four who spent their first seasons in the hills of East Tennessee. Journey with me for a little while…

I grew up in a small town in east Tennessee. The beautiful rolling hills lay just outside the dusty curtains that hang haphazardly above my bedroom window. In the mornings, I was awakened by the sound of birds singing, the mournful moan of our red-bone hound dog, Bum, and the sound of my mother bangin' pots in the kitchen as she scrambled eggs and fried sausage. I could tell exactly when it was time to get up, 'because I'd smell the biscuits browning.

My summer days consisted of fighting with my younger sister, Angie, then playing games with her. We knew those hills like our own backyard, for that is just what they were. We played '*Lost in Space*' (she always got to be Judy because of her blonde hair), hide and seek, freeze tag, bicycle races, stomped through muddy creek beds, caught butterflies, lightening bugs, frogs, crawfish. We simply enjoyed life. A simple life. We lacked for nothing and wanted everything. I remember laughing loud and often. I remember jokes, smiles, music. I remember the way my father smelled on Sunday morning before church. I remember how beautiful my mom looked in her red suit.

I remember so many things; still others are reduced to images, feelings, smells. They are triggered by the strangest things. Going on a field trip with my son, sitting on his bus, I was carried back to another bus, thirty years before. The seats stuck to my legs in the same way. The bus driver peered through the overhead mirror in the same manner; you know that kind of searching-scowl that all bus drivers develop over time. I was suddenly six years old, on my way to school. I felt the same little rush, the empty feeling in the pit of my stomach. I shook my head to clear the deja vu webs.

I lived in a butterscotch-colored house on a dirt road called Walls Hollow. My dad built the house after our trailer burned down one night while we were at the stock car races. Does that sound redneck enough for you? I loved our butterscotch house. I never asked why daddy painted it that color, but looking back, I feel reasonably certain that the paint must have been a good deal. Back then I just thought it was beautiful. I felt calm when I looked at that house. I felt safe living in that house.

When my Papaw was pouring our concrete sidewalk he let all of us girls, four at that time, put our hands in the wet cement. Four perfect little handprints sealed in time. It was fun then; it makes me cry now.

A year or so ago I went back to the old house. The new owners had changed everything. The house had been enlarged, outbuildings added. My old basketball goal was now home to a couple of cars. The garden my daddy had planted every year was gone, the yard swing absent as well. A couple of things remained, however. Wonderful things that called me back again, to a time that now exists only in my mind.

Sitting beside the kitchen door was the dogwood tree I had loved as a child. In the springtime, it had large white blooms with crimson edges. My mother had stood with me at that dogwood tree and shared the story of how the bloom represented the cross of Christ. I remember how tenderly she held the flower as she explained its legend. I remember her hands. I look at my own hands now to see hers. They are the same.

As I approached the walk, I was almost afraid to look. Thirty years had come and gone since papaw had knelt with us, pressing chubby fingers into wet, gritty cement. What if they had erased the handprints? Would proof of my childhood also be erased? I wanted so badly to see the four tangible imprints of my lost youth. I walked slowly, eyes shut tight as I approached the place where they had once been. I took a deep breath, counted to three, tilted my head forward and opened my eyes.

They were there!

I exhaled.

They were just as they had been thirty years earlier. Their imprint more shallow, yet undeniably there.

I knelt beside what I felt almost an effigy of the little girl I had been. My now wrinkled, dishpan hand, trembled as it cautiously traced the edges of a much smaller one. I looked at my sisters' hands beside my own and flashes of a lifetime skittered through my mind. Tears, unchecked, spilled from my eyes as I mourned the loss of those tender, innocent years, then those tears were replaced by tears of triumph as I realized that all four of these little hands still led full, blessed lives. Not one of those children had been lost over the years. They all still loved one another, still played 'house' together - only for real this time, still spent holidays together, still rambled through the unchanging, beautiful hills of East Tennessee.

They all still laughed - loud and often.

Season's change. Our Strong Father does not.

Questions or comments concerning today's lesson:

Day 3

Changing Plans

"My days have passed, my plans are shattered, and so are the desires of my heart."

Job 17:11

"Commit to the Lord whatever you do and all of your plans will succeed."

Proverbs 16:3

What do you think these scriptures mean?

_____
_____
_____
_____

Now, look at Proverbs 19:21.

It will be the Lord's plan that prevails. I am so glad! Want to know why? Because I know what His plans are, and I would not miss them for the world – literally!

"For I know the plans I have for you," declares the LORD, "plans to prosper you and not to harm you, plans to give you hope and a future. Then you will call upon me and come and pray to me, and I will listen to you. You will seek me and find me when you seek me with all your heart. I will be found by you," declares the LORD, "and will bring you back from captivity. I will gather you from all the nations and places where I have banished you," declares the LORD, "and will bring you back to the place from which I carried you into exile."

Jeremiah 29:11-14

I like His plans much better than the ones I make.

If you are like me, you have probably made a lot of plans in your life and seen many of them fall through. You have wished, hoped, and then been disappointed when things did not go as you had *planned*. We have all been there. Does that mean we should never plan anything again? No. It simply means that our plans should always come in line with His plans for us. How do we know if they line up? We ask Him. He is still a God who speaks to His children. You have His last will and testament. You know what His desire for your life is because He laid it all out in His will. When you start making plans, see what God has to say about it before you set anything into motion.

I once had a friend who loved to say, "It's easier to get forgiven than to get permission." I strongly disagree. I want permission so there will be nothing to have to forgive!

When was the last time you asked God about His plans for your life? What did He tell you? Before you say "nothing," try to remember if you really listened or if you did all of the talking. If you did all of the talking, stop right now and ask Him again, then spend a little time (or a lot) listening for His voice. He is interested and He does have input.

What did He say?

_____
_____
_____
_____
_____

Have your plans changed lately? Are you in a place you did not expect to be? I know I am! If so, please explain.

_____
_____
_____
_____
_____

Why do you think God is allowing the unexpected to happen in your life?

_____
_____
_____
_____
_____

I have a sneaking suspicion that it has something to do with **James 1:2-4**:

> *"Consider it pure joy, my brothers, whenever you face trials of many kinds, because you know that the testing of your faith develops perseverance. Perseverance must finish its work so that you may be mature and complete, not lacking anything."*

I know you have heard the saying, "That which does not kill us makes us stronger." I would suggest to you, however, "that which we commit to God makes us stronger." Our walk with Him demands we lay down all before Him. Our plans, our dreams, our hopes should all be placed at His feet so that He may hand back to us only the things that line up with His plan for us.

My husband is a very wise man (though I find it quite difficult to admit at times). For as long as I have known him I have considered him the smartest man I know. He is honest, forthright, honorable and devout. Because he always seems to have it together, I try to pay attention when he tells me what God is saying to him. One time I asked him about a particularly difficult time in his life and he encapsulated his answer in this way: "It was as if the Lord picked me up by my ankles and shook all of my priorities out of my pockets. He then said, *Pick them back up in the order in which I tell you."*

This statement had such an impact on me. I do not want God to have to shake me to get at my plans and priorities. I want to give them to Him and have Him line them up as He wills. I then want to follow closely behind Him and listen for His step-by-step instructions. To hear a still, small voice, you must follow very closely.

What are your plans for the rest of the week?

___

Have you consulted God about your plans? What did He have to say about it?

___

Read Proverbs 3:5, 6.

Make Him part of everything you do. His plans for you are beyond your wildest dreams!

Questions or comments concerning today's lesson:

Day 4

Changing Relationships

"Now this is our boast: Our conscience testifies that we have conducted ourselves in the world, and especially in our relations with you, in the holiness and sincerity that are from God. We have done so not according to worldly wisdom but according to God's grace."

2 Corinthians 1:12

I remember the first time I held my oldest son in my arms. As tears poured from my eyes and laughter tumbled from my lips, I beheld a face more precious than any I had ever known. This tiny person that lay naked upon my chest was the embodiment of every mothering fantasy I had ever indulged in. He smelled like life renewed and carried in his tiny clenched fist the absolute key to my heart. I never dreamed that one heart could hold that much love. When they brought him into my hospital room in the wee hours of the morning to be fed I thought I must surely be the most blessed woman in the world. I held him close and nuzzled his downy neck, kissed his rosebud lips and smelled his hair. I became enthralled with this little heart-stealer. I remained in my state of parental bliss for quite some time. Through toddler twos, and first school days, I hung upon his every word. He was most assuredly the smartest, funniest, most talented child in the world. Then something happened…

This baby boy became a preteen. Yes, I hear the moans of sympathy at this very moment. All of you moms are finding common ground here. I just know it. Anyway, this baby boy became six-foot-tall overnight with an independent streak that matched his stature. Those rosebud lips could come up with some of the most taciturn replies you could ever have the displeasure of hearing. He became so disagreeable when he decided he knew everything there was to know about the world. Far be it from his parents to try to contradict him. I think what hurt the worst was that I did not think I was as "everything" to him as he was to me. My opinions did not matter anymore. So, with the onslaught of his new attitude, came the change in our relationship.

The child I had once wanted to be with continuously now precipitated my hasty departure from whatever room he happened to enter. I would honestly retreat from my own child. I did not fear him, I dreaded him. I knew that if we were together for very long we would end up in some sort of strife and I did not see the benefit in that for either one of us. I had never had a preteen and did not know what to do with one, so I was hoping to leave the fray until the battle was over or a cease-fire had at least been negotiated.

Several years have passed since that harrowing eighteen-month period, and I now want to be with my child again (his younger brother, on the other hand, is treading upon a very familiar battleground). As his hormonal level balanced out, so did his temperament. He is once again a pleasure to my heart. He is funny, talented and smart, just as I knew he would be when I first gazed upon that face. We had to go through relational changes to get here, but it was worth every moment.

In the same manner, God goes through all of our changes with us. He loves us the same whether we are in a lovely or unlovable phase.

When in your life do you think you loved Jesus most? Why?

_____
_____
_____
_____

Do you think your relationship with Christ has changed over the past year? If so, how?

_____
_____
_____
_____

If you could change one thing about your relationship with Him, what would that change be?

_____
_____
_____
_____

Do you remember when you were saved? Tell a little about it in the space provided.

_____
_____
_____
_____

How has your relationship with Christ changed since the day of your salvation?

_____
_____
_____
_____

I hope all of you were able to get something very positive out of answering the questions above. I wanted you to see that even though you may not see the growth and change on a daily basis, there is growth and change nonetheless. We are constantly evolving in our relationships with the Lord and with one another. We go through changes and phases that make us lovable at times and unlovable at others. Ultimately, the changes will either bring us closer or drive us apart based on where our focus remains during that change.

Do you remember the action figures that came out a few years ago called, *Transformers*? These toys transformed from one thing into another completely different thing, then back again. Many parents really disliked them, but I am using them for creative illustration at this moment. Let's just say you had two of these toys and you set their wheels in motion and aimed them toward a predetermined destination. As the transformers moved forward, they changed shape and their function altered from what it had previously been. Their ultimate destination, however, did not change. They both arrived at their destination looking nothing like they did when they started out.

We are quite similar in our journey toward perfection. If we are following the ultimate predetermined destination, all of the transforming and changing will still not alter our course. We arrive very differently than when we started, yet, arrive we do. So, the next time you see someone changing before your eyes, recognize that he is in transition, but still headed in the same direction you are. Give friends the room they need to grow and change. Let your spouse become everything that God intends for them to be without falling apart when he is not what you expected. Make allowances for those who transform more slowly or do not look beautiful in the process. We will all arrive at the feet of our Father one day and the changes we have gone through will be nothing in comparison to the change we will make at our ultimate destination.

> *"Listen, I tell you a mystery: We will not all sleep, but we will all be changed - in a flash, in the twinkling of an eye, at the last trumpet. For the trumpet will sound, the dead will be raised imperishable, and we will be changed."*
>
> 1 Corinthians 15:51-52

Let the changes come!

Questions or comments concerning today's lesson:

Only Yesterday

It seems like only yesterday, mottled red face pinched,
Flailing tiny fists upraised, into this world you inched.

Like purest cotton sprang unruly curls on perfect head,
Close examination confirmed what mom thought, it was red!

I thought surely the heavens would quickly miss this one so rare.
I looked into your little face and worried, "Oh, do I dare?"

I kissed your fuzzy cheek, the softest down my lips would meet.
New life's aroma filled my senses, sweet calm, so replete.

I peeled back pastel blankets to reveal ten perfect toes.
I searched angelic features, saw a handsome button nose.

Puckered lips , brow furled in frown, sublime picture you did make.
I thought, *Oh Lord, My heart's so full. It's more than I can take.*

You stretched and compact body became, oh, I'd say, inches long.
Five fingers curled round one of mine and squeezed. *He thinks he's strong.*

The first night you lay in my arms, I knew what joy true was.
Fair baldhead, sweet cheeks so red, and neck of downy fuzz.

Well, love, years have flown, you're almost grown, this mother's heart is torn.
No more fair head. Feet hang off the bed. A man these years have borne.

When I pass you in the hallway, I often fight the urge,
To scoot to side, let you pass by, and say, *Excuse me, sir.*

I often think to myself, *How can I bear to see him leave?*
I find my heart in my throat, hand soon tugging on your sleeve.

"Mama needs a hug," I say. You hold me close, so near.
I think, *Oh Lord, I love him so. Why can't he just stay here!*

No woman will be good enough, for my son, don't you know.
I squeeze a little harder, 'til strained voice says, "Mom, let go."

Precious few the years we have to protect beneath our roof,
To kiss skinned knees, to pull from trees, to hear the lispy tooth.

Memories, each day are made be them great or fair.
Of late, I find myself at bedside, thanking God you're there.

So hard to think of babes in arms, holding babies of their own.
It comes so fast, the future past, my little boy's full-grown.

Forgive me for mistakes I've made, while learning as I went.
For ballgames missed, boo-boos not kissed and special time not spent.

If I could do it over, I know just what I would do
I'd never waste a moment of the time I had with you.

Each time I got the chance to sit and talk to you, I would.
I would make less of mistakes you'd made, and emphasize the good.

I would tell you each and every day, how blessed you make me feel.
I would spend the time with you each night, beside the bed to kneel.

I would sing to you each morning, a song your day to start.
I would hold you on my lap and pray, I'd share complete my heart.

Still, there's no returning to beginnings we've begun,
Still, we can pray, that God will make the best of what we've done.

That is where I am now Aaron. I have placed in you, my best.
But when times get tough, you feel like giving up, and you face another test,

Turn to the one who knows much more than I could ever teach.
He loves you more than life itself, and He has a grander reach.

He loaned you to me for a time, but His you truly are.
Like oceans wild and skies of blue and brightest shooting star.

A purpose you were placed here for, seek Him to find your course.
Needs you have, that man can't meet. He alone will be your source.

Trust Him, Son, He's faithful. He will never let you go.
Love Him, Son, He's worthy. In wisdom you will grow.

Take Him to your bosom. Place His words upon your head.
Talk with Him in wee hours when you're lying in your bed.

Laugh with Him, Rejoice in Him. Make Him your Father true.
For there will never be a parent who can love as He loves you.

I'm thankful for my time with you. My days will empty be.
When baby boy, his mother's joy, leaves hearth and home and knee.

I'm always here, sweet baby dear. My arms will always hold,
Though tall you be, at six foot three, a son is never too old,

To crawl into his mother's lap, and sit for moments rare,
Recalling sweet, perfect tiny feet, and downy cotton hair.

I love you, my sweet Son.
You are a precious gift from God!

Written for my boys, Aaron & Matthew.

Questions or comments concerning today's lesson:

Day 5

Changing Hearts

"Create in me a new, clean heart, O God, filled with clean thoughts and right desires."

Psalm 51:10 (TLB)

Read I Samuel 1.

Hannah is a woman most of us have read much about over the years. Her story of grief turned joy, then the great sacrifice of obedience, has tugged at our hearts for some time. I mean, the very thought of finally having a baby when you have longed so for years, then giving him up! I cannot begin to imagine what she must have gone through. Still, I know this much, Hannah's heart was something special. Hannah had suffered much, loved much, received much and sacrificed much. She was strong beyond my perception of what a strong woman should be. This heart was obviously quite special to God, for He made it a point to share her story with us.

Today, I would like to look at some changes of the heart that Hannah went through, that we too must experience if we are ever to have a *noteworthy heart*.

Verses 5 and 6 tell us that Hannah's womb had been closed.

Have you ever felt like a part of your heart was just shut off from the rest of the world? Maybe you feel barren in an area of your life – as if you are not productive in anything you do. You see others around you producing fruit (like Hannah as she watched Peninnah), yet you see none in your own life. You may even have a Peninnah of your own who just loves to torment you. You have felt like a failure for so long, you cannot even remember what you felt like before this torment came along. We know that Hannah had suffered for some time (verse 7 says many years), long enough for her rival to produce much fruit.

Hannah had a longing in her heart and a broken spirit before the Lord. When everything finally came to a head and Hannah basically fell apart before the Lord. Even the man of God did not understand (see verse 14). There are times in our lives when no one will understand, save God. We will be broken and our souls will be wracked with bitter tears. In those moments it will be God alone who hears our cries and comes to our aid.

Please read the following scriptures and see what the Lord has to say about broken hearts and contrite spirits. Write your thoughts about each verse in the spaces provided.

Psalm 51:17.

_____
_____
_____

Isaiah 57:15.

_____
_____
_____

Isaiah 66:2.

_____
_____
_____

"The lamp of the LORD searches the spirit of a man; it searches out his inmost being."
Proverbs 20:27

On that fateful night when Hannah went outside to weep her tears before the Lord, God searched Hannah's innermost and received the prayers of a mother's heart. He saw her brokenness and moved with compassion upon her. I have often wondered if Hannah had not made her promise, would the Lord have honored her request. I somehow believe that He would have. I think he would have given her the child she so sought. I like to think that her offer of her son just pleased Him to the point of saying, "Okay then, because of your sacrifice, he will be one of my most prized."

Our bargains with God are not what prompt Him to stretch forth His hand, for it is our heart that speaks to Him, not our lips.

Hannah made the most important decision of her life during a "dinner party." There was no lightening bolt or thunderclap, and angels did not sing out prompting her to bring her heart to God. What she had was a heart that could take no more, a heaviness that had finally bowed her low, and a determination to lay it all out there for the Lord: to break before Him, so that He alone could put the pieces back together.

Look once again at verse 15 and fill in the blanks.

"I was _____ _____ my _____ to the Lord."

When Hannah says she poured out her soul, she is basically pouring out her mind, will and emotions. She is telling Him what has consumed her thoughts (mind), telling how badly she has longed to have a child of her own (will) and how deeply she has hurt because of her barrenness (emotions). She gives it all to Him. She admits her pain, her shame and her frustration. She runs to her Comforter in search of solace only He can give.

Some of us have carried open wounds in our soul for way too long. We have tried to nurse ourselves back to wholeness through a variety of methods, but none has succeeded. There is but one way to truly find healing and that is to lance the wound and allow the poison to be poured out. Only then will true healing begin. There is much at stake here. Your heart holds the issues of life. If you are confused about your life issues, there is impurity or disease in the heart that must be dealt with. You have a fear that if you ever truly let go, you will lose control.

Oh, but precious friend, that is exactly what is needed. A physician cannot operate if you keep your hands over the afflicted area. Neither will your Great Physician. He is the ultimate cardiologist and He longs to take away your heart of stone and give you a heart of flesh. He wants you to be able to love people again and to let them love you in return. He wants you to remove your hands from your wounded heart and give Him full access so that He may heal you.

Read Psalm 13:5, 6.

God is asking us to trust Him with our hearts again. When was the last time you really did?

_____
_____
_____
_____

What happened to make you close your heart both to Him and to those around you?

_____
_____
_____
_____

Do you think pain was the ultimate intent of your injury or perhaps there was a greater purpose? What about isolation and desolation?

_____
_____
_____
_____

What might be gained through your trusting God with your heart again?

_____
_____
_____
_____

What might be lost through keeping your heart from Him?
_____
_____
_____

Write a prayer asking God to show you areas that you have kept from Him. Give Him full and complete access so that your healing may begin.
_____
_____
_____
_____
_____
_____
_____

Start over with an empty heart that He will fill with good things.

Questions or comments concerning today's lesson:

Nothing to Offer

I have nothing, Lord, to offer You.
My hands are empty.
Anything I might ever attain would be as nothing before You.
I try and try to be good,
To reach the point of miserably less than perfect,
Only to find that I am miles away from even that poor measure.

I have nothing, Lord, to offer You.
I wonder at times if You did not look closely enough...
before choosing me.
Yes, Father, I know nothing eludes You,
Still, at the risk of belligerence, may I please ask why me?
Did You see something in me that I have yet to see?

I have nothing, Lord, to offer You.
My faith weakens when provoked,
My hands fail to perform the most menial of tasks when prompted.
I see all of the wondrous works You do through others,
What have I to give My Master in return for this good fortune?
How can I repay what I do not understand?
Father, I am bowed by the awesome grace I have received.

I have nothing, Lord, to offer You.
This, then, I suppose, must be what I offer...
Nothing...
Nothing of the old me that wallowed in pride and pity,
Nothing of the shell that purposed to find her own way in this world,
Nothing of the shadow I used to be.
Nothing of the faithless, angry creation I was before you found me.
Oh Lord, I have nothing to offer You,
Please receive my nothing and make it something in Your hands.

CLASS NOTES

Week Ten

I Wish Someone Had Told Me All Things are Possible with God

Jesus looked at them and said, "With man this is impossible, but not with God; all things are possible with God."

Mark 10:27

Day 1
Childish Dreams

Day 2
New Hopes

Day 3
Setting Goals

Day 4
Mountain Moving

Day 5
Dare to Dream

When was the last time you allowed yourself to really hope for something? You know the kind of hope that makes it virtually impossible to sit still. Images of that which you are hoping for so fill your mind that you can think of little else. Do you remember what that feels like? Hope stirs the life within you, rekindles the flames of drive left dormant. True hope changes your countenance, motivates your actions, pervades your speech and invades your dreams. True hope is good for your heart. Having a dream or vision for your life adds purpose to your step, pushes your shoulders back and propels you forward unlike anything else. Where did you leave your dreams? When did you throw your hope away? Did you know that God's plan for you is one overflowing with hope for your future? This week we are going for the gold, reaching for the brass ring – recapturing the dream. This week will hear the rhythms of vision pounding in our hearts, for, my precious friend, all things are possible from God.

Day 1

Childish Dreams

"When I was a child, I talked like a child, I thought like a child, I reasoned like a child. When I became a man, I put childish ways behind me."

I Corinthians 13:11

I cannot believe we are already at the end of our study.

What once seemed impossible to me has now become a reality. God has truly taught me something through this time. He has taught me that I really can do anything if I just depend on Him and press through the barriers. When He first spoke to my heart and prompted me to write this study, sharing my heart with all of you, I must admit that I questioned God in my spirit. I thought He must surely be mistaken in choosing me to do this.

I mean, I am the one who has a propensity toward giving up on even the small stuff. How could he possibly think I could complete a study compiled of 50 lessons? I was doing well to actually attend a weekly study, much less write one.

Still, here we are, about to actually finish what we started. All I can say is that I have found Him faithful. He has walked me through every step of this process, and in doing so He has opened up a whole world of possibilities; things I had not dared dream about for years.

When I was a little girl, one of my favorite shows was "The Walton's." It was simple, honest and filled with kids like the ones I went to school with. My favorite part of the whole show, however, was always the last part. That was when John Boy would go to his room and write about the day. I use to imagine that I would one day write eloquent words that told about my life in the hills of Tennessee. As the Walton family called out their signature goodnights, I was reaching for my journal, pretending that I, like John Boy, was a *real* writer. Thursday nights. Eight O'clock. Me and John Boy.

Not a fancy dream, a simple dream, but my dream nonetheless. Years later, I have come to realize that it was not so much a dream as recognition of who I was on the inside. My dream was a voice calling from my spirit, prompting me toward the writing gift that God had placed inside of me. He gave me dreams that lined up with His plan for my life.

More than likely, he has done the same with you. Your dreams may well be the prompting of the Holy Spirit toward your particular calling or gift. In finishing this study, I have completed something that was out of my realm of possibility, but well within His plan for me. God is teaching me every day that the boundaries I have set for my life are not necessarily His boundaries. He is calling all of us to take a leap of faith and begin to believe Him for the big stuff - the things we used to dream about, but now seem totally out of our reach. You used to dream big. You used to have hope. God is calling you to run the race again, to hope *again*.

Why does being a grown-up mean that you have to let go of your dreams?

_____
_____
_____
_____

Was there ever a time when you were going all out toward your long-time dream? If so, what happened?

_____
_____
_____
_____

Was God involved in your plans? Did you ever ask Him if your dream was His plan for you?

_____
_____
_____
_____

How does it make you feel to begin even thinking about those dreams and goals you used to have?

_____
_____
_____
_____

For many of you the slightest thought of those old dreams makes you feel funny on the inside, as if you should not even be thinking about those dreams because you are only setting yourself up for disappointment. Who told you that? Did God tell you to lay them down? If He did, then by all means do not even go there. However, if you have yet to hear from Him on those dreams, run to Him and ask Him what He thinks.

Never let your reason for giving up be that it was too hard. The only legitimate reason to lay something down is that it is out of God's plan and will for your life. If you do not ask Him, you will never know.

A scripture that really helped me when I was going through a difficult time with hopelessness (a lack of dreams) was **Galatians 5:7, 8**. Let' turn there and take a look.

Please write the scripture in the space provided.

_____
_____
_____
_____

You were running a good race. You were doing a good job. You had hope. You were focused and determined. Who (or what) cut in on you? What stopped your dream? What kept you from doing what you believed was right?

Take just a few moments and think about the questions this scripture raises. Ask God to show you where your dreams fell to the side, and write the answer below. It may take more than the short time set aside for your study today, but I ask that you ponder these things for a while. Ask the Lord to show you when things changed. Then ask Him to renew your dreams – the ones that He alone wants you to have.

_____
_____
_____
_____

The next part of the verse says it all.

> *"that kind of persuasion does not come from the one who calls you."*
>
> Galationa 5:8

God does not steal your hopes and dreams. He gives every good and perfect gift. When your life is dedicated to the pursuit of Him, your dreams become gifts from Him. Do not let anyone take them away.

Questions or comments concerning today's lesson:

Day 2

New Hopes

"Life will be brighter than noonday, and darkness will become like morning. You will be secure, because there is hope; you will look about you and take your rest in safety."

Job 11:17, 18

When did the Lord last speak to your heart concerning your future? When was the last time you asked Him for clear direction concerning where you and your family are headed? What did He tell you?

_____
_____
_____
_____

Today I want to focus on one thing and that is the stirring up of hope on the inside of you.

Read Job 6:11-13.

Have you ever been there? Are you there now? You can almost hear Job's latent hope as he asks, and I paraphrase "Do I have any power to help myself? How in the world can I possibly do anything right when all around me has become a testimony of failure?" He has lost sight of his hope, but there is still a glimmer of the hope of truth within him. He has lost everything, but there is something inside of him that calls him to hope again, something that will keep him from absolutely giving up and crawling under a rock to die. That something is not actually a *what*, but a *Who. Christ in us, the hope of glory,* propels us forward and helps us to lift our head when our flesh wants to quit. Even at Job's lowest moment, hope still dwelt on the inside of him because God was with him.

God is with you at this very moment. You need only speak His name to have the embers of hope fan into flame within you. Why?

Read Isaiah 10:17 and Hebrews 12:29.

You call on His name, and you are calling down fire from heaven! That fire is an all-consuming fire. Our God comes in and burns up all of the dead works that have led to hopelessness, and there is once again room for real hope!

What do I mean by "dead works that lead to hopelessness?" These are the things that we have hoped in other than God. Maybe it was a friend you turned to instead of God, or a diet that only proved once again that you were a failure. These things drain us and never give anything back. Sometimes these are even the things that we thought we were doing *for* God, but He never even had a say in the matter. With each failure, we thought we had missed God, but it was not Him we were actually pursuing, so how could we have missed Him? Motivation can make a world of difference.

When we place our hope in anyone or anything other than Him, we can expect to be disappointed.

What was the last thing you placed your hope in that caused disappointment?

_____
_____
_____
_____

My last thing was a diet. It is amazing to me that even now, knowing better, I still expect to get different results from the same old thing. Diets will not set you free from a bondage birthed in your spirit. Only God can truly free you from the bondage of weight. It is a heart matter. Trust me, I am learning this one the hard way.

Still, whether yielded to in my own life or not, the Truth is still the Truth. God's Word is the only place we should ever place our hope. Anything else is a chasing of the wind

> *"I have seen all the things that are done under the sun; all of them are meaningless, a chasing after the wind."*
>
> Ecclesiastes 1:14

and a tossing to and fro by *winds of doctrine* (see Ephesians 4:14).

How do you do it? How do you get your hope onto what (or into Whom) is true?

You have to make a decision to believe again. You cannot birth hope unless you first believe that He is your hope. Then everything becomes possible again. When you begin to take Him at His Word, you can once again let hope rise within you, for He will not disappoint you.

> *"And hope does not disappoint us."*
>
> Romans 5:5

We see this principle of faith bringing hope played out beautifully in the book of Mark. As you read the following scripture passage, keep in mind the fact that this father has been through everything imaginable with his child. I am sure he has exhausted every resource concerning the boy's deliverance. His hope has probably run down to the very last drop. Still, he hears about this man called Jesus and hope begins to stir within his breast. He catches a glimmer of the light at the end of the tunnel. The following passage (when you read between the lines) is the story of renewed hope. It is a story that can be played out in your own heart today.

A man in the crowd answered, "Teacher, I brought you my son, who is possessed by a spirit that has robbed him of speech. Whenever it seizes him, it throws him to the ground. He foams at the mouth, gnashes his teeth and becomes rigid. I asked your disciples to drive out the spirit, but they could not."
"O unbelieving generation," Jesus replied, "how long shall I stay with you? How long shall I put up with you? Bring the boy to me."
So they brought him. When the spirit saw Jesus, it immediately threw the boy into a convulsion. He fell to the ground and rolled around, foaming at the mouth. Jesus asked the boy's father, "How long has he been like this?"
"From childhood," he answered. "It has often thrown him into fire or water to kill him. But if you can do anything, take pity on us and help us."
"'If you can?'" said Jesus. "Everything is possible for him who believes."
Immediately the boy's father exclaimed, "I do believe; help me overcome my unbelief!"

Mark 9:17-24

Everything is possible for Him who believes. Everything! Set your hope on the truth of those words. They are words spoken directly from the mouth of Jesus. He would never lie to you. He is "not a man that He should lie." Hope again! Look forward to your life again. Wake up in the morning expecting something wonderful to happen. Be excited about what God has in store for you. Look around every corner with anticipation. Enjoy your life! It is the only one you get on this planet (contrary to what some may believe).

My Hope Is Set

I will fix my gaze upon My Love,
Will trust in Him alone,
My hope shall be in the Fairest One,
Until He brings me home.

I dare not turn my heart away,
This world does steal so much,
But I will stay close by and know,
My Shepherd's gentle touch.

Keep me near, Lord, to your heart,
Draw me to Your side,
Forever safe and quite secure,
My life in You to hide.

For now, Strong Warrior, I'm content,
To love You in this place,
Still, my hope is set upon the day,
I'll love You face to face.

My hope is set on nothing less…

What are you setting your hope on today? In what area of your life do you need God to renew your hope?

_____
_____
_____
_____

Ask Him to minister to you in these specific areas today. I am praying for you.

Questions or comments concerning today's lesson:

Day 3

Setting Goals

"Are you so foolish? After beginning with the Spirit, are you now trying to attain your goal by human effort?"

Galatians 3:3

Okay, we have now looked back at some of our dreams we had put aside. We have asked the Lord to show us if those old dreams were part of His plan for our lives and asked Him if it was okay to pick them back up again. Once we received the go-ahead, we asked Him to renew our hope; to stir the embers of hope that we had allowed to die down. We have begun to place our trust in Him again, and believe His Word to build our faith. Now what do we do?

We begin to set reasonable goals.

If you are still waiting for your answer from the Lord concerning the old dreams, it is still okay to go ahead with today's lesson. Even if the Lord tells you to lay down the old in favor of the new (He does that quite often), you still need to know how to proceed with whatever the Lord gives you.

1. Pray, pray, pray…

Read the following scriptures and match them to the promise given.

Ephesians 3:17	**Sure salvation**
Matthew 26:41	**Where to go, what to do**
Jeremiah 29:12	**He will listen to you**
2 Corinthians 13:7	**Safety from temptation**
Jeremiah 42:3	**You will do nothing wrong**
Psalm 69:13	**Rooted and established**

Everything must be grounded in prayer. Direction, safety, instruction, all comes into your goal setting when you start with prayer. Not just a whisper here or there, but actual substantial time spent in communication with the Father. Jesus will be right there interceding as you seek God concerning the setting of goals for your future.

When He speaks…

2. Write everything down.

Impressions. Words. Truths. When the Lord begins to speak into your life (and He will if you ask

Him, giving Him the opportunity by getting quiet before Him) write everything down. This is for a couple of reasons;

a) you can check it out with the Word of God to make sure everything lines up with the infallible truth of the Word, and

b) so you will not forget the Word of the Lord. I know, you are probably saying 'forget the Word?' How could I possibly do that?

> *"Listen then to what the parable of the sower means: When anyone hears the message about the kingdom and does not understand it, the evil one comes and snatches away what was sown in his heart. This is the seed sown along the path. The one who received the seed that fell on rocky places is the man who hears the word and at once receives it with joy. But since he has no root, he lasts only a short time. When trouble or persecution comes because of the word, he quickly falls away. The one who received the seed that fell among the thorns is the man who hears the word, but the worries of this life and the deceitfulness of wealth choke it, making it unfruitful."*
>
> Matthew 13:18-22

There are many scenarios where the Word can be snatched from you. Write it down (a book of remembrance) and hold on for dear life. Satan does not want you to know the will of God concerning your life; it brings too much hope to your spirit and he will do anything to make you let it go. Keep the truth before your eyes so that you may remind the enemy of God's plan for your life (he really dislikes that!).

3. Take Baby Steps…until you are strong enough to run.

Baby steps require complete reliance on the one who is standing waiting for you at the other end. You can rely on the One Whom you are headed toward. As He bids you forward, just do it. Do not wait until you have the whole agenda laid out in front of you, but move forward by degrees. Just as you did not lose your way by all of a sudden drastically rebelling against His will, neither will you find yourself in immediate perfect alignment with it. You strayed away from your dreams little by little. Therefore, you must also give yourself time and extend grace to yourself during the process of learning to walk according to His will again.

This is the point in your *hope process* at which the enemy would love to stop you. You have renewed your dream, been given hope and now you are ready to start walking with purpose toward the fulfillment of that dream. He wants you to stumble here so that he may kick you while you are down.

Baby steps.

You fall down.

You get up.

You fall down. You get up. Eventually you walk with surety and you begin to see a clearly defined destination. You fall down. You get up. You walk forward again.

So, remember:

1. Pray without ceasing.

2. Write a book of remembrance.

3. Baby step, allowing the extension of grace.

> *Jesus looked at them and said, "With man this is impossible, but with God all things are possible."*
>
> Matthew 19:26

You can do it! Christ in you, the Hope of Glory, will strengthen you for the task ahead. Tomorrow we will talk about moving those mountains out of your way.

Questions or comments concerning today's lesson:

Day 4

Mountain Moving

He replied, "Because you have so little faith. I tell you the truth, if you have faith as small as a mustard seed, you can say to this mountain, 'Move from here to there' and it will move. Nothing will be impossible for you."

Matthew 17:20

"Say to this mountain..."

It is hard to speak to a mountain if you do not see the mountain before you. Recognizing and naming the mountains you may face in your pursuit of God's will for your life will be our agenda for today. We will expose some of the volcanoes that have remained dormant, but are set to erupt in your path should you neglect their removal.

Mount I've-never-been-able-to-do-this-before

This mountain rises before many believers. The echoes from the hilltop cry, "It didn't work the last time. What makes you think it will work this time?" This mountain reminds you of every time you have tried in the past and failed.

Has his unfailing love vanished forever? Has his promise failed for all time? Has God forgotten to be merciful? Has he in anger withheld his compassion? Selah

> *"Then I thought, To this I will appeal: the years of the right hand of the Most High. I will remember the deeds of the LORD; yes, I will remember your miracles of long ago. I will meditate on all your works and consider all your mighty deeds."*

Psalm 77:8-12

The deeds of the Lord, not your own, should be your focus.

Say to this mountain, "It is not about whether or not I have failed; I know that I have. It is about the fact that God's promise never will. Yes, I have failed, but God will not fail me, and you will not stop me!"

Mount You-don't-deserve-a blessing

This mountain is the home of the poor-pitiful-me clan. This is where all would-be self-martyrs go to bury themselves. This mountain's echo goes something like this, "Oh, no. Don't worry about me. I don't need any dreams or goals. Just give me an old shack in the corner of heaven."

> *"I am still confident of this: I will see the goodness of the LORD <u>in the land of the living.</u>"*
> Psalm 27:13 (emphasis mine)

We do not have to wait until we arrive in heaven to enjoy the goodness of the Lord. He wants to give us good gifts while we are here (see Matthew 7:11 and Luke 11:13). He is our Father, and it is His will to bless His children, sharing those things that will fill and complete their lives. I believe having dreams would definitely fall into that category.

> *"Where there is no vision, the people perish."*
> Proverbs 29:18 (KJV)

God never intended for His children to lose their dreams. Our God-given dreams help propel us toward His ultimate plan for our lives. Everyone deserves to have a dream.

Say to this mountain, "The plans of the Lord stand firm forever, the purposes of His heart through all generations (Psalm 33:11). I will not give up on His plans (and blessings) for me! Mountain of lies be gone!"

And finally, we face the biggest mountain of all…

Mount What-must-I-do?

This mountain has long been the homestead of the I-will-work-my-way-into-heaven family. This family has built churches, taught Sunday school classes, paid tithes and even clothed the naked and fed the hungry. The echo of this mountain is "I will do it…I will Do it…I will *Do* it." The problem with the people on this mountain? They are exhausted. Time in intimate relationship with the Lord would be considered down time and they do not allow themselves that luxury. Reading the Word and praying seem much too passive. Besides, that just seems a little too easy. "Remember," comes the battle cry from this mountaintop, "faith without works is dead!" They seem to have forgotten a basic truth that would set them free from their perpetual motion.

Turn to Ephesians 2:8, 9.

According to the passage you have just read, what should you say to this *Do* Mountain?

_____
_____
_____
_____

You really can move beyond this mountain range. You have the words to bring them down right on the tip of your tongue. Funny thing though about these mountains, they like to pop up out of nowhere every once in a while. That is why the book of remembrance we spoke of in yesterday's lesson is so important. Keep a record of God's faithfulness in mountain removal so that you may send that mountain back to its rightful place – under your feet, not in your path!

Now, when you stand atop that mountain, let go with a shout of victory that will remind all of those who tread close-by of the goodness of the Lord. Know that you have been assuaged on the mountain.

I too have found satisfaction on mountaintops of my own.

Name your mountain(s) in the space provided (be creative).

_____
_____
_____
_____

What will you say to your mountains (each one, respectively)?

_____
_____
_____
_____

Questions or comments concerning today's lesson:

A Psalm of Assuage
(To be sang upon the mountain)

Cry out, cry out, wounded soul,
Wells of pain release.
Fall, Oh fall to knee, hearts pride,
Trade folly great for peace.

Tender, tender mercies find,
Rain, sweet rain of tears.
Perfect, perfect spirit calm,
Transcending lifeless years.

Faithful, Faithful, Father He,
Children run and see.
Play, Oh play in splendid bliss,
Loose dark chains, be free!

Done, it's done! Battle be gone,
Victory's scent is sweet.
Rest, Oh rest, fair Presence found,
Tears bathe the Master's feet.

Sing, Oh sing, of faith renewed,
The mountain's been made straight.
Tread, do tread on level ground,
Through dreams of old pried gate.

The mountain is only as big as your fear.

Day 5

Dare To Dream

"And Joseph had a dream."

Genesis 37:5

No more mountains. There are no obstacles standing between you and your goals and dreams. It is a clear shot. Might take a while to get there, but you can actually see it again. You can almost smell the fresh air; almost feel the cleansing winds. You are beginning to imagine what the view will be like from your soon to be attained vista. Your heart pounds a little harder – higher altitudes have a way of doing that to a person – and you are beginning to actually think differently. Great. Wonderful. Couldn't be better.

Oh, yes it can!

God has more for you that you ever dreamed possible. He did not bring you to this point to show you the view of the valley. He brought you here to show you your next mountaintop in the distance. He brought you here to birth in you a hunger to go further, to dream bigger dreams. God has brought you to this place to show you once and for all that there is nothing too big for Him, and that if you will just believe Him, nothing is impossible for you.

Read Luke 1:37.

I want you to list three things that you have considered to be impossible in your life. It may be a ministry you think will never come to pass, a life-companion you do not believe you will ever meet, or maybe even a weight loss you long to achieve. Whatever it is, write it down.

_____
_____
_____
_____
_____
_____
_____
_____
_____

One day you will look back and this will be your book of remembrance. God is going to begin to make the impossible seem possible. God is going to begin to move among His people in ways we have only read about until this time. We are going to walk in the miraculous, live in the extraordinary. God has promised us that in the last days He was going to pour out His Spirit upon all flesh. Let's look at this passage together.

> *"In the last days, God says, I will pour out my Spirit on all people. Your sons and daughters will prophesy, your young men will see visions, your old men will dream dreams. Even on my servants, both men and women, I will pour out my Spirit in those days, and they will prophesy. I will show wonders in the heaven above and signs on the earth below, blood and fire and billows of smoke. The sun will be turned to darkness and the moon to blood before the coming of the great and glorious day of the Lord. And everyone who calls on the name of the Lord will be saved."*
>
> Acts 2:17-21

My fellow pilgrims, we are here but for the briefest time. Soon our Lord will come for His Bride. All of the time we have upon this earth should be spent in preparation for that glorious appearing. The mountains we bring down will be mere stepping-stones on our journey toward Him. The battles we fight are as pebbles thrown by the enemy in lieu of that day. Tears that have been shed will flow into that river of life to join with that of all of the sainted ones before us. Our suffering will give way to joyous laughter; our troubles melt into sublime peace. All that has gone before will be as nothing; small trophies to place at His feet.

There is coming a day...

> *"Then I saw a new heaven and a new earth, for the first heaven and the first earth had passed away, and there was no longer any sea. I saw the Holy City, the new Jerusalem, coming down out of heaven from God, prepared as a bride beautifully dressed for her husband.*
> *And I heard a loud voice from the throne saying, 'Now the dwelling of God is with men, and he will live with them. They will be his people, and God himself will be with them and be their God. He will wipe every tear from their eyes. There will be no more death or mourning or crying or pain, for the old order of things has passed away.'*
> *He who was seated on the throne said, 'I am making everything new!' Then he said, 'Write this down, for these words are trustworthy and true.' He said to me: 'It is done. I am the Alpha and the Omega, the Beginning and the End. To him who is thirsty I will give to drink without cost from the spring of the water of life. He who overcomes will inherit all this, and I will be his God and he will be my son.'"*
>
> Revelation 21:1-7

Dare to dream my friend. Dream big! He is a big God and He is Your God.

One day your faith will become sight. You will see your dreams realized as the eastern sky splits in two and our Faithful One comes in all of His Glory to claim that which belongs to Him.

Until that day,

I will dare to dream...

> *"I saw heaven standing open and there before me was a white horse, whose rider is called Faithful and True."*
>
> Revelations 19:11

You were made in His image, my sister.

Dare to dream.

CLASS NOTES

Afterword

There is a wonderful song entitled, "I Could Sing of Your Love Forever." Truly, I could sing (or write) of His wonderful ways, through my prose, upon page after page. To find a place to end this pouring out of spirit matters is impossible to a heart that would love to continue the journey. There is still so much to share. I have yet to arrive at empty. I had believed that all would be spent upon the pages you have just read, but I was not taking into consideration the constant refilling done by the Precious Holy Spirit as we pour ourselves into the lives of others. The journey continues, and shall continue until the day my last breath is drawn upon this earth.

It is my sincere desire to never stop learning, never cease growing in knowledge, and to continually seek His wisdom in all things. I pray that you, too, will desire this in your own life. Our Precious Father has so very much in store for His children. May we press ever forward until we reach the place where His perfect will is all that we desire.

May our lives be ever poured out before our merciful Lord and Savior, Jesus Christ.

Thank you for taking this journey with me.

I pray we travel together again…

Soon!

In His Love,

About Barbie Loflin

The founder of *Poured Out Ministries*, **Barbie Loflin** serves as Assistant Pastor of Springhouse Worship & Arts Center, a creative, thriving, multicultural body of believers just outside of Nashville, Tennessee. An author and composer, her work has appeared in New York Times best sellers, and can be found in bookstores across the nation.

Barbie lives with her husband Hal in middle Tennessee. They have three grown children, Aaron, Matt and Kayti.

Also Available From
WordCrafts Press

Morning Mist
Stories from the Water's Edge
by Barbie Loflin

Positioned for Transition
Arrows in His Hand
by Barbie Loflin

Why I Failed in the Music Business
and how NOT to follow in my footsteps
by Steve Grossman

Youth Ministry is Easy!
and 9 other lies
by Aaron Shaver

Chronicles of a Believer
by Don McCain

Illuminations
by Paula K. Parker & Tracy Sugg

A Revelation of Love
by Jill Grossman

Pro-Verb Ponderings
31 Ruminations on Positive Action
by Rodney Boyd

www.wordcrafts.net

www.ingramcontent.com/pod-product-compliance
Lightning Source LLC
Chambersburg PA
CBHW081353290426
44110CB00018B/2366